THE WAY

Student's Book

Second Edition

THE WAY, THE TRUTH & THE LIFE SERIES

By Sr. Marcellina Cooney CP

Editorial Team

Jonathan Bindloss, Angela Grady, Stephen Horsman, Liz McCaul,
Dominic Marshall, Paul Moloney, Rachel Smith and Mary White

Teachers' Enterprise in Religious Education Co. Ltd
Catholic Truth Society

Introduction

Welcome to this edition of 'The Way' which will be complemented by 'The Truth' and 'The Life'. In St. John's Gospel, Jesus calls each one of us individually and, together, as Church, to live in him, who is the 'Way, the Truth and the Life' (Jn. 14:6).

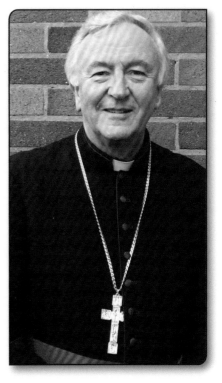

In 'The Way' you will unfold the Sacred Scriptures and be invited to explore the beauty, call and promise of God revealing Himself in the Old Testament and, most fully in the New Testament in His Son, Jesus Christ.

This is a challenging enterprise because you have to discover a new way of thinking about what you are learning in Religious Education – it is called theology. You have to think in a deeper way and look for meanings that are not immediately obvious. You will even be starting with Revelation and Faith!

As you progress in your study, you will come to a much deeper understanding of who Jesus is, what Jesus' love (grace) is and does for us. You will have the opportunity to explore new ways of thinking about the Church as the 'People of God' and as the 'Body of Jesus Christ'. It is in and through this relationship with Jesus that you will discover the power of the sacraments and how to live out the help which they offer us.

God calls all people to Himself and when you study the unit on other faiths I invite you to deepen your understanding of them and to take initiatives to build bonds of friendship with many young people you will come to know.

I hope that in your studies this year you will grow closer to Jesus in faith, hope and love and that you will discover the promise his call holds for you.

✝Vincent Nichols

✠ Vincent Nichols
Archbishop of Westminster

Contents

Big Questions

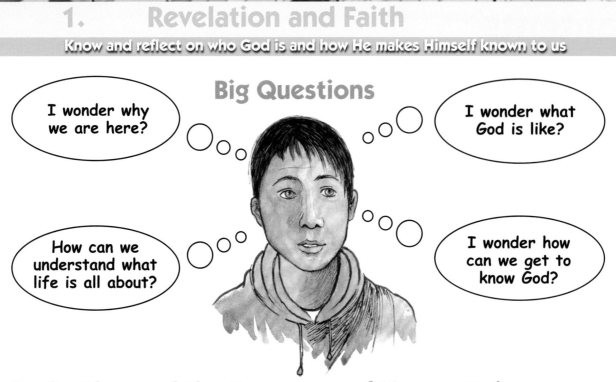

I wonder why we are here?

I wonder what God is like?

How can we understand what life is all about?

I wonder how can we get to know God?

God's Plan and the Response of Human Beings

God's Plan

In this unit, we will learn how God gradually revealed Himself to us and how He began to build a relationship of faith and friendship. This is not just a story of something which happened long ago; it is still happening. By finding out how this divine revelation began and developed, we will come to understand God's wonderful plan for us.

Revelation

The word 'revelation' comes from the Latin meaning to 'unveil' or to make known.

> **By Divine Revelation we mean God making known Himself and His plans for us. God is love, as St. John says in his First Letter (1 Jn. 4:8). Revelation is the way in which God communicates this love to us in order that we can share in His life. This is what we call Divine Revelation.**

The story of mankind's relationship with God begins with God's call to Abraham. Abraham was searching for God. However, he had to wait until God chose to break into his life and reveal that He had a plan for him. God said, "Leave your country and your kindred and your father's house and go to the land that I will show you" (Gen. 12:1). God didn't give Abraham details of His plan. God required Abraham to have faith in Him. He asked him to leave the life he had known and journey to an unknown country.

Faith in God is a supernatural gift. It is a free gift of God and is available to all who humbly seek it. Our faith continually grows through listening to the Word of God and opening our hearts to Him so that we can receive HIM.

Pause to Reflect

Every faith journey begins
with God knocking at the door of our heart.
That knock can take many forms:
a spiritual hunger,
an inspiring person,
a loving friend.

Our faith journey continues
with God walking with us every step of the way.
God lights our path when it grows dark.
God lifts our spirit when it wanes.
God helps us up when we stumble and fall.
God's grace embraces us every inch of the way.

But God respects our freedom.
God does not force us.
This means that if God's grace
is to touch and transform us,
we must open ourselves to it.
We must work as if all depends on us,
but trust as if all depends on God.

Mark Link SJ

Activities

1. a) Explain what is meant by Revelation and Faith.
   b) Why do you think Revelation and Faith have been put together in this unit?

2. List some of the things you believe about God through faith.

3. Try to think of a person you know who has a strong faith in God. Explain why you have chosen this person.

KEY WORDS: supernatural, transform

Abraham:
A Man of Faith

Over the following years, God spoke to Abraham and challenged his faith many times. Each encounter increased Abraham's knowledge and strengthened his trust in God. Gradually God revealed His plan to Abraham and gave him many blessings. Like Abraham, we too are searching for God.

If we have faith and trust in Him, God will break into our lives and reveal His wonderful plan for us so that we can have a deep and lasting relationship with Him.

Abraham had great faith in God. He had to face many big tests and only discovered after a very long time the plans God had for him.

Abraham's family lived about four thousand years ago – they were shepherds and they moved around a great deal. They had already moved from Ur, which was probably in modern Iraq. Then they went to Haran, which was in Turkey. Abraham had come to understand that God loved him and wanted him to respond to that love. He understood that even though he had been used to thinking about many gods, even worshipping things like the moon, God wanted Abraham to belong to Him alone. What a challenge for him!

The more Abraham responded to God's love, the more God revealed about Himself.

God's Challenge

One day, Abraham realised that God was challenging him to make a very big commitment. He understood that he had to leave his father's house and even the land of Haran where he had come to feel at home. He had to trust God and set out for a land which God would show him (Gen. 12:1-8).

This was the promise God made to Abraham as he set out with Sarah his wife, Lot his nephew, and some others in the family. God said:

"I will make of you a great nation, and I will bless you, and make your name great, so that you will be a blessing. I will bless those who bless you, and him who curses you I will curse; and by you all the families of the earth shall bless themselves" **(Gen. 12:2-3).**

For some time, Abraham and his wife wandered through the land of Canaan. Abraham never forgot the promise God had made to him, but he grew more anxious as time went on. He was a foreigner, without land and his wife had no children, and now she was well past childbearing age. How could he become the father of a great nation without any children of his own? It seemed a total contradiction. He had to remember that God is always faithful to His promises and to trust completely in Him.

Activities

1. **Use the diagram your teacher will give you.**
   In the first three boxes write a summary of Abraham's journey of faith using bullet points.
   You will complete the diagram after the next lesson.
   - **Faith: what was Abraham's first act of faith?**
   - **Challenge: what was difficult about it?**
   - **Blessing: what did God promise?**

2. a) **What do you think people put their faith in today?**
   b) **What are some of their idols?**
   c) **What can we do to ensure that we do not worship false idols?**

3. **If you were Abraham:**
   a) **how would you have answered God's call?**
   b) **what do you think you would have gained?**
   c) **what do you think you would have lost?**

God's Covenant with Abraham

A covenant is a solemn promise made between two people or groups of people. The covenant is made when the people accept it and undertake to fulfil their part of it.

When Abraham was very, very old, God appeared to him again and made a covenant with him.

"I will make a covenant with you," God told Abraham.

"This is what you must do. I am God. You must believe in Me and only worship Me. You must walk in My ways and live as I ask."

"This is what I shall do. I shall keep this covenant I have made with you. I shall give you many descendants and you will be the father of many nations... . The covenant I have made with you will last forever... I shall call you by the name of Abraham, and your wife will be called Sarah from now on. I shall bless her and give her a son..."

"Sarah will have a baby, and she will call him Isaac. Then I shall keep the covenant I have made with Isaac, just as I said."

Abraham fell on his face and laughed. The thought of his wife having a baby, when she was well past child-bearing age, was just too much (Gen. 17:1-9, 15-19, 21).

Activities

a) What does God promise Abraham?
b) In return, what must Abraham do?

KEY WORD: descendants

Sarah Hears God's Promise to Her

Not long afterwards, Abraham was resting in the shady doorway of his tent during the hottest part of the day. As he rested, he became aware of three men standing in front of him.

Abraham's family were always kind and welcoming to strangers. Abraham jumped up and ran towards the three men. He bowed low to welcome them.

"Please," he said politely, "do not continue your journey until you have rested. Let me have water brought to you. You can wash your dusty feet and sit under the shade of the tree to rest. I will bring a little bread to you which you can eat before you go on." The men agreed to this and Abraham hurried into the tent to find Sarah.

"Quickly", he said, "make some flat bread for our guests." Then he ran out to his herd of cattle and chose a calf, which his herdsman killed and prepared.
When everything was ready, Abraham took the food and some milk and brought it out to where his guests were resting under the tree. He gave them the food and the conversation continued while Sarah listened behind the door of the tent:

Abraham and Sarah had both laughed at how God said He would keep His promise to make them the parents of a great nation. They were well beyond the age for having children. Even though they had spontaneously laughed at the idea of having children, they did believe and put their faith and trust in God's Word. They had a son, Isaac. This was the son in whom "all nations of the earth would be blessed" (Gen. 21:1-6).

1. Complete the next section of your diagram:
   • **Faith:** what was the covenant Abraham had to believe in?
   • **Challenge:** what was difficult about it?
   • **Blessing:** how was God's promise to be fulfilled?

2. a) What does the story of Abraham reveal about God?
   b) What does it tell us about Abraham?

3. In groups, role-play different parts of Abraham's experience:
   • **God's challenge**
   • **Experience in the desert**
   • **God's Covenant**
   • **Three visitors**
   • **Abraham & Sarah talking about the promise of a son.**

4. "You must walk in my ways," God said to Abraham and also says to us. Give examples of how you can live this out.

Know that when God asked Abraham to sacrifice his only son, He was testing his faith. Reflect on the meaning of this story for us.

Abraham's Faith is Tested

Some years after the birth of Isaac, Abraham's faith was put to the test again.

God said to Abraham:

"Take your son, your only son Isaac, whom you love, and go to the land of Moriah, and offer him there as a burnt offering upon one of the mountains of which I shall tell you."

God's request is painfully clear – *"Take your son, your only son Isaac, whom you love…"* It is hard to understand, totally incomprehensible! How can God give him a child and then ask him to sacrifice him? The pain that goes through Abraham at the thought of sacrificing his son is unbearable – but Abraham is a man of faith. In silence, he obeys God.

"Rising early next morning Abraham saddled his donkey and took with him two of his servants and his son Isaac. He chopped the wood for the burnt offering and started out on his journey to the place God had pointed out to him."

After three days, they reached the place. The suffering was even greater as "Abraham took the wood for the burnt offering, loaded it on Isaac and carried in his own hands the fire and the knife".

Isaac was puzzled.
"We have the wood and the fire," he said, "but where is the lamb for the sacrifice?"

"God will provide the lamb Himself," answered his father and they walked on together.

At the top of the mountain, Abraham built an altar, laid the wood on it and then tied Isaac to the altar. He raised the knife. In all his long and difficult life, this must have been the longest and most difficult moment. He must have wondered how God meant to keep the covenant with Isaac now.

But God always keeps his promises. Abraham trusted God completely.

"Stop! Don't hurt the boy. I know you trust me," God told Abraham.

Abraham looked round – close by them was a ram caught by its horns in a bush and he took the ram as a sacrifice instead.

"Because you have done this," God said, *"and have not withheld your son, your only son, I will indeed bless you. Your descendants will be as many as the stars of heaven and as the grains of sand on the seashore. All the nations of the earth shall bless themselves by your descendants, because you have obeyed My voice"* (Gen. 22:1-18).

Activities

1. **In pairs, look back through the story of Abraham and list the times when God's ways seemed to contradict common sense.**

2. **Abraham's life was one of FAITH. Make a 'mind map' of the key points when his faith was tested.**

3. **HOT SEAT**
   In pairs, come up with five or more questions to ask Abraham, Sarah and/or Isaac about the near sacrifice of Isaac.
   The teacher picks three pupils to be in the 'hot seat'. The rest of the class ask them questions.

What does this story reveal about God?

It show us that:

- God chose Abraham freely out of love for him.
- God keeps His promises which He makes out of love.
- All God wants is an open heart. Abraham's extraordinary faith means that his heart remained open to God.
- God looks at the heart rather than external sacrifices.

What does this story tell us about Abraham?

- Abraham responded with total faith in God.
- He was willing to face up to all the uncertainties that the future held for him.
- He believed in God's words even though they seemed to contradict common sense.

What can we learn from this Story?

- God helps our faith to grow by challenging us.
- God knows what is in our hearts.
- God always does what is best for us even if we do not understand it at the time.
- God will reward our efforts to love and serve Him.

Abraham is called our father in faith because we are all invited to respond to God with faith like his.

Activities

1. **Complete your diagram:**
   - **Faith: why did God test Abraham?**
   - **Challenge: what was he asked to do?**
   - **Blessing: what was it?**

2. **Now study the diagram carefully and weigh up your responses to see which was the greatest:**
   - **Abraham's faith;**
   - **the challenges God sent;**
   - **the blessings God gave him.**

3. **Choose one of the bullet points from the section 'WHAT CAN WE LEARN FROM THIS STORY':**
   a) Explain how it challenges you.
   b) Explain how it helps you.

4. **"Is Abraham a man of faith or a fool?" Discuss.**

Know that David was chosen by God to be a great leader.
Reflect on David's response to God's call.
Reflect on our own response.

Choice of Leaders

What do people look for when they want to choose leaders?

Some will look for intelligence, experience, ability to inspire others and qualifications. What do you think are the qualities that God looks for in the people He chooses? To find out, we are going to look at Jesse and his eight sons.

David is Chosen

Over a long period of time, many leaders were chosen by God to guide the Chosen People, for example, Moses, Aaron, Samuel and King Saul who was now getting very old.

God knew that Saul was not a faithful king and he sent the prophet Samuel out to anoint the next king. Samuel invited a man called Jesse and his sons to a special sacrifice he was offering to God. He asked for all of Jesse's sons to come to him. When he saw what a fine man the first son was, Samuel thought: "Surely this is the next king". But God spoke inside Samuel's heart.

"Do not look at his appearance or at his height, because I have rejected him; I do not see things the way you do. You can only see his appearance, but I can see his heart."

So Samuel looked at all the other sons, but he received no sign from God about any of them. He asked if there were any more.

"You have seen all except the youngest," answered Jesse. "He is in the fields, looking after the sheep." Samuel asked for him and as soon as he saw David, he knew this was the next king, chosen by God. David was anointed. He received the Spirit of the Lord with total trust.

Activities

1. **Discuss which outward appearances are important: to you; your family; your school; your friends.**

2. **"The Lord sees not as man sees: man looks on outward appearance, but the Lord looks at the heart' (1 Sam. 16:7). What is the Bible teaching us about outward appearances?**

KEY WORD: anointed

13

David's Faith is Tested

Soon afterwards, David spent part of his time serving King Saul. At this time, God's chosen people were at war with the Philistines and before long the two armies were facing each other, ready for battle. From out of the Philistine ranks strode a huge man – almost a giant. His name was Goliath. Goliath stood and shouted to the ranks of Israel:

"Who will come out and fight me? If you can find a man to beat me, we will all be your servants, but if *I* beat *your* man, then *you* will be *our* servants!"

At this, King Saul's men were afraid. Who could beat a man as huge as that?
Goliath came out every morning and every evening for forty days. Each day he issued his challenge but no one took it up.

Some of David's older brothers were in the army. While David was talking to them, he heard the shouting of Goliath.

"Who is this man who defies God's people?" David asked.

"I will go and fight this Goliath," he said to King Saul.

Saul was not happy about this,

"This Goliath has been a fighter all his life," he said. **"You are just a young lad."**

David shook his head, **"I may be young, but I have killed bears and lions in the wilderness when I was minding the sheep. God helped me then and He will help me now"** (1 Sam. 17:33-37).

What happened next?
Open your Bible and read 1 Sam. 17:40-50

When Goliath saw David, he was scornful. But David said,
"You come to me armed with a sword and a spear, but I come to you in the name of

God and I shall strike you down so everyone will know about the God of Israel."

David was not as weak as he seemed to Goliath – but he could never have beaten him in a hand-to-hand fight. Instead, he trusted God to help him. His faith was strong. He took a stone from his bag, put it in the sling, whirled it round his head and hurled it. The stone hit Goliath in the centre of his forehead and he fell to the ground dead.

The account of David and Goliath reminds us that we will have to overcome difficulties in our lives by placing our trust in God as David did.

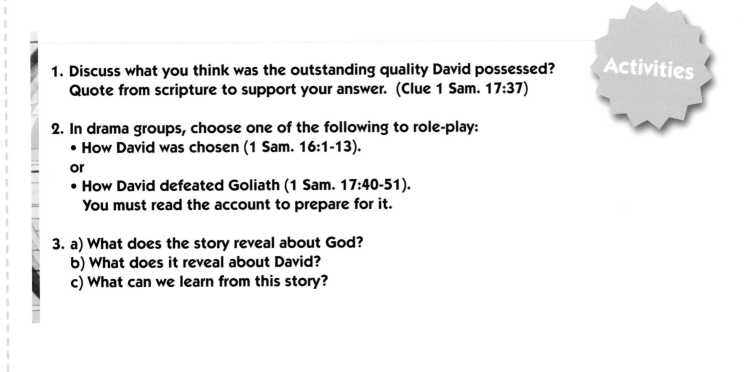

Activities

1. Discuss what you think was the outstanding quality David possessed? Quote from scripture to support your answer. (Clue 1 Sam. 17:37)

2. In drama groups, choose one of the following to role-play:
   • How David was chosen (1 Sam. 16:1-13).
   or
   • How David defeated Goliath (1 Sam. 17:40-51).
     You must read the account to prepare for it.

3. a) What does the story reveal about God?
   b) What does it reveal about David?
   c) What can we learn from this story?

Pause to Reflect

Some people strive to be **Goliaths** in life. For example, the Goliaths are those who strive to be big, throw their weight around, intimidate others with words, actions, text messages.
God asks us to be Davids.
Why? In what way can you be like David in your life?

God's Promises

David achieved one military triumph after another but now time had passed, Saul was dead and David was king himself. To begin with he was a good king. His first thought was to build a temple for the Ark of the Covenant where God's laws were kept – a house for God. But God had different ideas. He made a covenant with David. He promised to:

· make David's name great;
· give him peace from his enemies;
· build him a house - a dynasty, or family line which would bring God's love to all nations. The house of David was going to last forever (2 Sam. 7:1-18).

David's Downfall

David had lived a very successful life but he became proud of his achievements and relied on himself, forgetting what God had done for him.

One day, David was walking on his rooftop in the late afternoon. The rooftop was flat and it overlooked other buildings. David saw a very beautiful woman bathing, and he sent a servant to find out her name. He found out she was called Bathsheba and she was the wife of a man called Uriah. Uriah was away fighting in a war for King David.

David arranged for Bathsheba to come to his room. David knew that he should not do what he wanted to do but thought that no one would find out about it. But the woman became pregnant. David was now faced with a situation he had not foreseen. He had thought he knew how to handle everything but now he was no longer sure.

Tormented by his dilemma, David called Uriah and gave him a letter to give to the commander of his army. This is what it said: "Put Uriah in the front of the hardest fighting, and then leave him, so he will be killed."
It was not long before David and Bathsheba heard that Uriah was dead. After a while they

KEY WORD: Ark of the Covenant

were married and a son was born to them. David thought he had got away with it, but God had not forgotten. He sent the prophet Nathan to David, and this is what Nathan told him.

"There were two men," Nathan said, "one was rich and the other poor. The rich man had flocks and herds of animals, but the poor man had only one – a little ewe lamb. He was very fond of this lamb. It grew up with his children, he fed it with bits from his own plate and hugged it close to his heart – he loved it so much.

One day, a traveller arrived and the rich man wanted to offer him a meal. He could have chosen any one of his own lambs from his flocks, but instead he took the poor man's lamb and had it killed and cooked."
David flew into a rage against the man and said to Nathan,

"This man deserves to die! He had no pity at all on that poor man. He should repay him four times over!" Nathan said to David, **"You are the man"** (2 Sam. 11 and 12:1-10).

Activities

1. **What was Nathan trying to teach David through this story?**

2. **How do you think David reacted when Nathan said, "You are the man"? Answer by sketching his face and using thought bubbles.**

David Repents

Nathan confronted David with his sinfulness and said that God would punish him for his evil deeds. David immediately turned to God, opened up and confessed his guilt: **"I have sinned before God"**. This sorrow came from his heart. He accepted responsibility for his actions, not only against the innocent people whose lives he had destroyed, but also against God who had done so much for him.

David repented and prayed:

"Have mercy on me, God, in your kindness.
In your compassion blot out my offence.
O wash me more and more from my guilt
and cleanse me from my sin.

My offences truly I know them:
my sin is always before me …
A humbled, contrite heart you
will not spurn" (Ps. 51:1-3, 17).

**What David discovered
through his sinfulness was
that God will not despise a
contrite and crushed heart.
This is what David passed on
to all future generations.**

What does God reveal to David?
- **Here, God is revealing his merciful love: God accepts people as they are even in their sin, if only they open their hearts to God.**

What can we learn from it?
- **That God's kind of love is merciful.**
- **God unconditionally accepts the person as he/she is.**
- **God may not approve of what the person has said or done but God still accepts the person. God still loves the person.**
- **On our part, we learn that we should open our hearts to God, no matter what we may have said or done.**

We know we have the Sacrament of Reconciliation which gives us the opportunity to express our sorrow for what we have done wrong and receive the power of God's forgiveness for ourselves.

1. a)   Study the temptations that may have taken place in David's mind.
   b)   Work in pairs and write out what his inner voice of conscience should have replied.
   c)   On your own, write out the reasons you think David would have given for the decisions he made.

Temptations

- I'm a great person.
- I'm a king I can do what I like.
- She's beautiful and she must be mine.
- I'll be careful, nothing will happen.
- I killed the giant.
- I know I can cope on my own.
- No one need know.

Inner voice of conscience....?

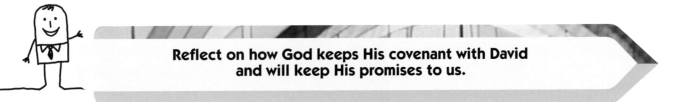

Reflect on how God keeps His covenant with David and will keep His promises to us.

Solomon's Dream

When King David died, one of his young sons, Solomon, became king after him.

One night, Solomon had a dream. God spoke to him in the dream and asked him what gift he would like to be given.

Solomon said to God, "You have given this land and this nation to my father David, and now to me. You have shown us so much love. But here I am, in the middle of this great nation, and I am like a little child. I don't know what to do or how to do it. Please, give me wisdom so I shall rule your people wisely and fairly."

God was pleased that Solomon had not asked for anything for himself.

"I shall give you what you have asked for," God said in the dream. "You will have wisdom. But I shall also give you what you have not asked for. You shall have riches and honour and, if you keep my commandments, you shall have long life also."

"And Solomon woke up" (1 Kings 3:4-15).

KEY WORDS: conscience, wisdom, commandments

Pause to Reflect

- What did Solomon ask for from God?
- What did God give him that he did not ask for?
- What gift would you like to ask God for? Why?

Solomon Uses His Gift of Wisdom

Soon afterwards, he was asked to solve a difficult problem – one that called for all the wisdom he had.

Two women came to him. Each had a very new baby, but one of the babies had died in the night. Each of the women said that the living baby was hers and that the dead one belonged to the other woman. King Solomon thought for a moment.

"Bring me a sword," he said. And a sword was brought. The King looked at each of the women.

"Both of you claim the living baby as your own," he said. **"Very well, you shall have half each."** And he said to the servant with the sword, **"Cut the living child in two and give each woman one half."**

At this, each of the women said something different. The first woman said, **"No! Don't do that! Let her have the baby!"**

The second woman said, **"That's fair – the baby won't belong to either of us. Cut it in half!"**

When he heard this, the King said, **"Don't kill the baby - give it to the first woman - she is its real mother."** And everyone was amazed at his wise judgement. (1 Kings 3:16-28).

So Solomon lived for many years. He ruled wisely and the land was peaceful. Solomon became very wealthy and he built the Temple to be the House of God, just as the prophet Nathan had told his father so many years ago.

Nevertheless, Solomon loved many women from foreign countries and clung to them in love. He had many wives and these turned his heart away from God and from being wholly true to the Lord.

So the Lord said to Solomon: **"Since you have not kept My covenant, I will surely tear the kingdom from you and give it to your servant. Yet for the sake of David your father I will not do it in your days, but I will tear it out of the hand of your son. However, I will not tear away all the kingdom; but I will give one tribe to your son, for the sake of David my Servant and for the sake of Jerusalem which I have chosen. God always keeps his promises"** (1 Kings 11:4-6, 11-13).

After Solomon's death, the kingdom split in half. The northern part was known as Israel and the southern part as Judah.

Key Points to Remember:

- God reminded the people of His love, His covenants and His laws.
- The people responded to God's love – for a while.
- Then they forgot and became involved with false gods from other nations.
- God sent them a prophet to remind them of how they should act – and of His covenant love.
- The people were sorry and tried again.

Activities

1. a) **What problem did the two women bring to Solomon?**
   b) **How did he know who was the real mother?**
   c) **What was Solomon's downfall?**

2. **Your friend Joe used to do well at school but recently he has neglected school work, plays truant, goes out with a gang; he's in big trouble in school and out of control at home. He's miserable and feels he has no one to turn to; he thinks even God has rejected him and will never forgive him for hurting others.**

   Write an email to Joe to help him to turn back to God and others.
   Use all the knowledge you have of God's dealings with people to support your advice to Joe.

3. **Revelation & Faith: Complete the 'Summary' sheet which your teacher will give you.**

2. God's Promises Fulfilled

Know about the exile of the Chosen People. Identify similar aspects in the lives of people today.

Exiled, Lost and Alone

Exile means banishment, being driven from your home, or sent where you do not want to go. You give up control of your own life; your own story. The experience of being displaced, lost and homeless is widespread in the world today. The need to belong, to have a safe place, to have a home is deep within each of us.

A PERSONAL REFLECTION

"So I have a new name: Refugee.
Strange that a name should take from me
my past, my personality and hope.
Strange refuge this.
So many seem to share this name,
yet we share so many differences.
I find no comfort in my new name.
I long to share my past, restore my pride.
To show I too, in time,
will offer more than I have borrowed.
For now the comfort that I see,
resides in the old,
yet a new name I would choose,
Friend."

By Ruvimbo Bungwe (14 years old)

Activities

1. a) **Reflect on Ruvimbo Bungwe's experience.**
   b) **What does it make you think?**
   c) **What issues does the story raise?**
   d) **How does the reflection relate to situations today?**

2. a) **What is the difference between political refugees and economic migrants?**
   b) **Give examples of both.**

Exile of the Chosen People

The Jewish people understood the pain and loneliness of being exiled and their story is important to help us understand the history of God's Chosen People. We are now going to see what happened to them.

In the years following the reign of King Solomon, many Jews became complacent and turned away from God. They believed God would always look after them; He had promised to do so. They were His Chosen People and He had made a covenant with them. But many Jews were not keeping their side of the covenant. Their worship at the Temple was just an outward show, their hearts were empty of love for God and they did not keep His commandments. Some people thought they did not need God, they had a good life, plenty of money and possessions; this was all they thought about. The kings who reigned after Solomon were often cruel and unjust; they made bad laws and did nothing to stop poor people being sold into slavery.

God sent prophets to His people to tell them to change their lives and turn back to Him but the people ignored or imprisoned them and continued to live in ways which were against God's law.

What happened?

Meanwhile, Babylon, a kingdom to the east of Judah, had become very powerful. The Babylonians did not worship God; they were polytheistic which means they worshipped many gods. In 587 BC, Nebuchadnezzar, king of Babylon, led an army into Judah. The Babylonians conquered and destroyed Jerusalem and the beautiful temple of Solomon was razed to the ground. The richest and most important Jewish people were deported from their homeland and taken to Babylon.

To be taken away from their own land was a traumatic and painful experience for the Jews; they felt they had lost their identity; they were no longer a nation. Many thought God had deserted them, had broken His promise to care for them. They quickly forgot all that God had done for them in the past and gave up the practice of their religion.

Pause to Reflect

Today, many people in different parts of the world are uprooted from their homeland and become exiles because of conflict.

- In which part of the world are people suffering most today?
- Why are they suffering?
- What do you think is the cause of it?
- Let us look out for information in the media so that we can spend more time later on looking into this in depth.

The Faithful Jews

Fortunately, there were other Jews who refused to give up hope and remained faithful to God. They saw the exile as a punishment for all their evil practices. They knew they needed to repent and to return to the laws and customs of their fathers in order to keep alive the Jewish way of life for themselves and for their children.

It was at this time that God sent the prophet Isaiah with words of comfort to these people uprooted from their homeland:

"Comfort, comfort my people, says your God.
Speak tenderly to Jerusalem (the Jews),
and cry to her that her warfare is ended,
that her iniquity is ended" (Is. 40:1-2).

And again the prophet reassures the people that God is with them:

"Fear not, for I have redeemed you;
I have called you by your name, you are mine" (Is. 43:1).

"Behold, I have carved you on the palm of my hand" (Is. 49:16).

Isaiah and other prophets reminded the people that it was God who was with them. And as they suffered under the power of foreign nations, they came to understand their need for God. Whatever the Chosen People did or did not do, the simple fact was that God's loving gaze was always upon them.

"By waiting and by calm you shall be saved, and in quiet and in trust your strength lies" (Is. 30:15).

The faithful Jews were no longer complacent. Spurred on by these recent experiences they worked on their sacred writings, that we now call the Bible. They wanted to hand on these sacred writings to their children and grandchildren. It was at this time that the Jews built synagogues which became important meeting places for them. It helped them to form a community and to keep alive their sense of national identity as God's Chosen People.

Activities

1. a) Choose one of the quotations on page 24. Write it out.
   b) What does it tell you about YOU and GOD?

2. Use a diagram to list:
   a) reasons for the exile of the Jews;
   b) how the people felt in exile;
   c) the effects of the exile.

Reasons	Feelings	Effects

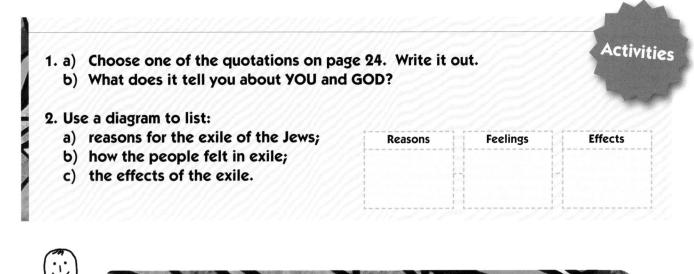

Know about the return from exile & God's plan for the Chosen People. Think about what they mean for us.

Return from Exile

When disaster or misfortune strikes it can have the positive effect of making us stop and think about all that has happened and what led up to it. Suffering can either harden our hearts or open them up in a cry to God for help. It was like this for the Jews in exile in Babylon.

So the prayers of the Jews who refused to give up hope, despite everything that had happened, were eventually and unexpectedly answered. In 537 BC, Cyrus, the Persian Emperor, conquered Babylon. The Jews who wished to do so were allowed to return to their native land. Many of those who had remained faithful to God returned to Jerusalem and began to rebuild it. There was great rejoicing even though Jerusalem had become a miserable hovel. The faith of these people in God had been tested and proved strong.

The suffering they experienced in exile made their religion more deeply spiritual, more a matter of the heart than it had been before.

The faithful men and women bowed low before God in total surrender. Their experience led them to understand that God's power is greatest and works best when people are aware of their own inadequacy. When people place their absolute trust in God, He is with them and works through them.

The Jews understood:

- It was not enough to worship publicly in the Temple; they had to live out what they believed.
- God had not failed to keep His covenant with them.
- God hears the prayer of the lowly and humble of heart.
- When we place absolute trust in God, we experience the greatness of His power.

Activities

1. Imagine you are the head of a refugee family: news has just come through that you can return home to your own land if you wish.

   Discuss:
   • reasons for returning;
   • reasons for staying.
   Consider different opinions within the family, for example, elderly members, children, teenagers.

2. If you were the head of this refugee family, what would be the most important factors that would influence your final decision? Write them down.

3. "God's power is greatest when we place absolute trust in Him".

   Work in pairs.
   a) Think about the Exile and your own experience of life.
   b) To what extent is this statement true?
   c) Give examples to support your answer.

God's Plan

Like many of us in times of difficulty and uncertainty, the Jews were anxious to find someone to protect them from their enemies, make wise laws and remind them of God's message. This is why they hoped for a warrior, a king and a prophet - but how, when and where they did not know.

Many people thought of the Messiah as a kind of national hero who would bring the people back to their land, rebuild the Temple and conquer all their enemies. He would be the one to bring peace to the world.

However, there was also a very different prophecy of the Messiah, one who would be a servant who would lay down his life for others. We will later see how these prophecies are reflected in the life of Jesus.

Prophecies

Here are some of the prophecies made about the Messiah approximately five hundred years before the birth of Jesus.

> "I will leave a remnant in your midst, a people humble and lowly, who take refuge in the name of the Lord" (Zeph. 3:12).

The prophet Isaiah had foretold that Israel would be reduced to a remnant and scattered to a distant nation. He compared Israel to a stump of a tree, but from it a branch would grow out of its roots:

> "There shall come forth a shoot from the stock of Jesse, and a branch shall grow out of his roots. And the spirit of the Lord shall rest upon him, a spirit of wisdom and understanding" (Is. 11:1-2).

> "Behold a young woman shall conceive and bear a son and shall call his name Emmanuel" (Is. 7:14).

> "O Bethlehem ... from you shall come forth for me one who is to be ruler in Israel" (Mic. 5:2).

> Isaiah said that when the Messiah comes "The people shall beat their swords into ploughshares, and their spears into pruning hooks. Nation shall not lift up sword against nation, Neither shall they learn war any more" (Is. 2:4).

KEY WORDS: Messiah, remnant, prophecies, stock of Jesse, ploughshares, Emmanuel

The Messiah would perform miracles:
"Then the eyes of the blind shall be opened,
and the ears of the deaf unstopped" (Is. 35:5).

"Then shall the lame man leap like a deer,
and the tongue of the dumb sing for joy" (Is. 35:6).

"The wolf lives with the lamb,
the panther lies down with the kid,
calf and lion feed together
with a little boy to lead them" (Is. 11:6).

"A voice cries: In the wilderness
prepare the way of the Lord,
Make straight in the desert a highway
for our God" (Is. 40:4).

The prophets showed how the promises made to God's people would be for all of us and the light of God's love would shine on the whole world.

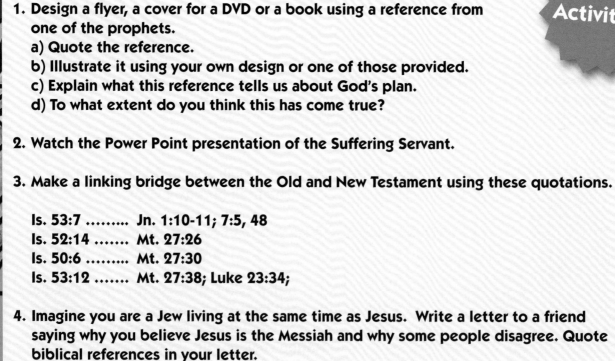

Activities

1. Design a flyer, a cover for a DVD or a book using a reference from one of the prophets.
   a) Quote the reference.
   b) Illustrate it using your own design or one of those provided.
   c) Explain what this reference tells us about God's plan.
   d) To what extent do you think this has come true?

2. Watch the Power Point presentation of the Suffering Servant.

3. Make a linking bridge between the Old and New Testament using these quotations.

   Is. 53:7 .... Jn. 1:10-11; 7:5, 48
   Is. 52:14 .... Mt. 27:26
   Is. 50:6 .... Mt. 27:30
   Is. 53:12 .... Mt. 27:38; Luke 23:34;

4. Imagine you are a Jew living at the same time as Jesus. Write a letter to a friend saying why you believe Jesus is the Messiah and why some people disagree. Quote biblical references in your letter.

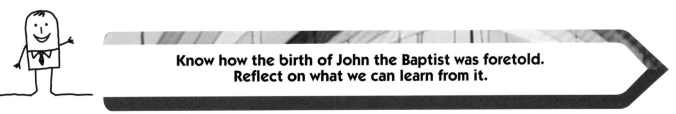
Letting Go, Letting God

It is when we hand over our lives to God that everything takes on a new meaning and life becomes an adventure but not one that we can plan. We will see:

- God can do much more than we believe;
- God can change our lives;
- God can give life.

It was like this for Zechariah and Elizabeth, an elderly Jewish couple, who faithfully observed all the Lord's commands.

Annunciation to Zechariah

Zechariah was in the Temple and went to light the incense when an angel appeared to him. He was overcome with fear when the angel said:

"Zechariah, do not be afraid, your prayer has been heard. Your wife Elizabeth is to bear you a son and you must name him John. He will be your joy and delight and many will rejoice at his birth, for he will be great in the sight of the Lord; he must drink no wine or strong drink. Even from his mother's womb he will be filled with the Holy Spirit and he will bring back many of the sons of Israel to the Lord their God" (Lk. 1:13-16).

Zechariah was confused, he could not believe such news and asked how he could be sure of it because his wife was well past child-bearing age.

"The angel replied, 'I am Gabriel who stands in God's presence, and I have been sent to speak to you and bring you this good news. Listen! Since you have not believed my words, which will come true at their appointed time, you will be silenced and have no power of speech until this has happened'" (Lk. 1:19-20).

Elizabeth accepted God's message with total surrender: " 'The Lord has done this for me', she said."

Zechariah must have been greatly shaken by the experience in the Temple.

If you were Zechariah:

a) How would you have felt?
b) What would you have done?
c) What do you think it would have done for your relationship with God?

Use bullet points to answer.

Activities

Pause to Reflect

- Zechariah had difficulty accepting what the angel said.
- He needed to grow spiritually if he was to be part of God's great plan.
- Imagine the absolute terror Zechariah must have felt when the angel said, 'I am Gabriel'. How would you have felt?
- His tongue was tied by God. He no longer had the power of speech and the angel was gone! What thoughts might have gone through his mind?

A New Beginning

Zechariah was alone again. The Angel was gone - but 'the end' marked 'a new beginning'. Zechariah had to **'let go and let God'** take over in his life. The end of the angel's visit was a new beginning in the relationship Zechariah had with God. The relationship did not depend on what Zechariah could **do** as a priest in the Temple but on his **opening his heart** to God and placing absolute trust in Him. He probably recalled the words of the prophet Isaiah:

"By waiting and by calm you shall be saved, and in quiet and in trust your strength lies" (Is. 30:15).

Just as it was for Zechariah, a time may come when God will confront us with something we have never planned or imagined. It is a little bit like this when God calls young people to serve him in a particular way through their vocation, for example, to be a priest, a nun, a monk, get married or be a lay missionary. Accepting God's plan for us brings happiness and fulfilment.

Activities

1. DRAMA:
   a) **In groups act out the scene of Zechariah in the Temple and at home with Elizabeth. Aim to show how the day unfolded.**
   b) **Choose to be one character from the scene. Write a diary entry showing your thoughts and feelings.**

2. QUIZ: Who else in the Bible had a baby in her old age?

KEY WORD: lay missionary

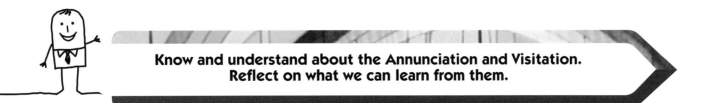

**Know and understand about the Annunciation and Visitation.
Reflect on what we can learn from them.**

Annunciation to Mary

In the mystery of the Annunciation, Mary is seen as the "model of faith". It is God who breaks into Mary's life. Mary does not go to God; it is God who comes to Mary through the angel Gabriel. He addresses Mary as "full of grace" or "highly favoured one". Mary is "greatly troubled": she thinks there must be some mistake. But the angel says:

"Mary, do not be afraid: you have won God's favour. Listen, you are to conceive and bear a son who will be called Son of the Most High." Mary asks, "How can this be since I am a virgin?"

Once again, she is reassured that God and God alone will do it all:

"'The Holy Spirit will come upon you,' the angel answered, 'and the power of the Most High will cover you with its shadow. And so the child will be holy and will be called Son of God'."

The angel then tells Mary that her cousin "Elizabeth has, in her old age, herself conceived a son, and she whom people called barren is now in her sixth month, *for nothing is impossible to God*".

Mary's only response is that of real faith. She is ready to let go of all her plans in order to let God be God in her life.

'I am the handmaid of the Lord,' she says. 'Let what you have said be done to me' (Lk. 1:26-38).

Activities

1. **Quiz: What was the difference between the response to the angel from Zechariah and Mary's response?**

2. **'Letting go and letting God take over' is probably one of the hardest things we have to do in life.**
   a) **How do you think we could prepare for such an experience? Think of something you could do every day.**
   b) **List some of the 'joys' and the 'hazards' of letting God take over in your life.**

KEY WORDS: model of faith, barren

The Visitation

Mary set out as quickly as she could to visit Elizabeth.

"Now as soon as Elizabeth heard Mary's greeting, the child leapt in her womb and Elizabeth was filled with the Holy Spirit. She gave a loud cry and said, 'Of all women you are the most blessed, and blessed is the fruit of your womb'."

The Magnificat

Mary is overcome with joy and says:

"My soul glorifies the Lord,
my spirit rejoices in God my Saviour.
He looks on His servant in her lowliness;
henceforth all ages will call me blessed.

The Almighty works marvels for me.
Holy His name!
His mercy is from age to age,
on those who fear Him.

He puts forth His arm in strength
and scatters the proud-hearted.
He casts the mighty from their thrones
and raises the lowly.

He fills the starving with good things,
sends the rich away empty.

He protects Israel, His servant,
remembering His mercy,
the mercy promised to our fathers,
to Abraham and his sons for ever"
(Lk. 1:46-55).

Mary stayed with Elizabeth three months and then went back home.

KEY WORDS: Visitation, Magnificat

Mary had to wait. She was certain that God would help her but had no idea where and when. She had to wait when Joseph wondered about her pregnancy and knew it was a big problem for him. She was certain that in God's good time all would be well, but for the moment it meant deep suffering, silence and surrender to His will.

Mary's experience helps us to discover God's mysterious actions:
· God turns the judgement of the world upside down.
· He comforts the lowly and terrifies the powerful.
· The humble, who completely trust in Him, are filled with good things.

Mary's Magnificat is a 'bombshell'; it is 'revolutionary'. It takes the standards of the world and turns them upside down.

Activities

1. **Mary decided to visit Elizabeth. When she arrived –**
   a) **What was her first experience? (Lk. 1:39-45)**
   b) **What prophecy did Elizabeth make?**

2. **What do you think the meeting between Mary and Elizabeth tells us about their babies - Jesus and John the Baptist as yet unborn?**

3. **Mary's Magnificat is revolutionary, that is, it completely changes the way we think about things.**
   a) **Study the Magnificat and pick out at least three ways in which it is revolutionary.**
   b) **How has this prophecy been fulfilled:**
      • **by Jesus;**
      • **by people in the world today?**

4. **Mary's prophecy has not been fully realised.**
   Do you agree?
      • **Say what you think and why;**
      • **give a different point of view and say why some people hold it;**
      • **say why you disagree with it.**

5. **Through Mary's words and life, God could revolutionise the way we THINK, ACT & LIVE.**
   a) **Think about the importance we attach to money, power, status, brains and good looks.**
   b) **In pairs, work out how God could change your life.**
   c) **How might this affect the way you live?**

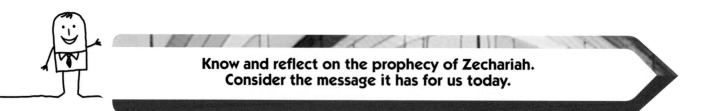
Elizabeth and Zechariah

The time came for the baby was to be named. According to custom, he should be called after his father Zechariah, but his mother objected and said, **"He is to be called John"**. The people were amazed and asked his father, who was still unable to speak, what he wanted him called.

"The father asked for a writing-tablet and wrote, 'His name is John'. They were all astonished. At that instant his power of speech returned" (Lk. 1:63).

All present were amazed and word soon spread all around the hill country of Judaea. The people treasured this experience in their hearts and wondered what this child would turn out to be. They were even more amazed when Zechariah, filled with the Holy Spirit, spoke this prophecy:

"Blessed be the Lord, the God of Israel!
He has visited His people and redeemed them ....

As for you, little child,
you shall be called a prophet of God, the most High.
You shall go ahead of the Lord
to prepare His ways before him,
to make known to His people their salvation
through forgiveness of all their sins,
the loving-kindness of the heart of our God
who visits us like the dawn from on high.

He will give light to those in darkness,
those who dwell in the shadow of death,
and guide us into the way of peace" (Lk.1:68-79).

KEY WORDS: redeemed, salvation

Zechariah's Prophecy

- For **Zechariah**, it reveals the new freedom, light and joy growing in his heart all the time when he could not speak. He had grown in the wisdom of letting God take over. The birth of his son brought about a spiritual re-birth in him.

- For **Elizabeth**, who was among the humble and lowly people who had always trusted in God, she knew that God was able to use her so that He could make known His astonishing plans for all of us.

- For the **people**, the prophecy was a puzzle: they were expecting God to send a Messiah who would be a political leader and would deliver them from foreign invaders.

Where are we in Zechariah's Prophecy?

John was born to make known the coming of Jesus.
- We are born **INTO** the life of Jesus.
- Today, we have to be prophets to **MAKE HIM KNOWN** to all people.
- **ADVENT** is the time of preparation.

Activities

1. Every phrase in Zechariah's prophecy is filled with meaning for us. Read it carefully again and answer the questions:
   a) What will John do for Jesus?
   b) What will he do for the people?
   c) What will he do for us?

2. ADVENT: Use a diagram like the one here.
   Put outside the circle all the ways you prepare 'outwardly' for Christmas, e.g. send cards. Inside the circle, write down all the ways you prepare yourself 'inwardly', e.g. receive the Sacrament of Reconciliation.

3. a) In groups, think of what you could do as a class or a school to make ADVENT special.
   b) Share your ideas with the rest of the class and reach a consensus on what to do.
   c) Draw up a plan of action.
   d) Write the plan into your own book and explain the purpose of it.

4. Create a personal ADVENT calendar to help you prepare to celebrate the birth of Jesus. In each box, write an action you could do each day, e.g. helping at home, giving money to charity, going to confession, forgiving someone.

5. TURN OFF, TURN ON
   a) Make a comparison between watching your favourite TV soap or film (at home) with watching a DVD on the Nativity (in school). After each write down:
      • what you felt inside;
      • what thoughts came to you.
   b) Write down the 'pros and cons' of both and draw conclusions on what was most helpful and why.

KEY WORD: Advent

God is Born: Why?

We recall that God created the world including the first man and woman. The first man and woman disobeyed God and their sin was passed down to all generations. Through our ancestors, Abraham, Moses, David and the prophets, God promised us a Saviour who would free us from our sins and give us eternal life with God forever.
This is why God sent His only Son into the world for us.

Christmas

When a baby is expected, the safety and comfort of the mother is top priority for all around her. For Mary and Joseph it coincided with a decree from Caesar Augustus that all the world should be enrolled. For them, it meant they had to set out on a long journey to Bethlehem, only to find that, when they arrived, there was no room in the inn. Our modern means of communication did not exist.

While they were there, the time came for Mary to have her baby.

"And she gave birth to her first-born son and wrapped him in swaddling clothes, and laid him in a manger, because there was no place for them in the inn.

And in that region there were shepherds out in the field, keeping watch over their flock by night. And the angel of the Lord appeared to them, and the glory of the Lord shone around them, and they were filled with fear. And the angel said to them, 'Be not afraid; for behold I bring you good news of great joy which will come to all the people; for to you is born this day in the city of David, a Saviour who is Christ the Lord. And this will be a sign for you: you will find the babe wrapped in swaddling cloths and lying in a manger" (Lk. 2:6-11).

KEY WORDS: swaddling clothes, Saviour

Pause to Reflect

- Who is this baby?
- Where is he born?
- Who welcomes him?

News Spreads

The shepherds made known what the angels had told them:
"Glory to God in the highest, and on earth peace among men with whom He is pleased" (Lk. 2:14).

King Herod was visited by wise men from the East who wanted to know more: **"Where is he who has been born king of the Jews? For we have seen his star in the East, and have come to worship him"** (Mt. 2:2).

Fear gripped Herod, his mighty power was threatened. He gathered all the chief priests and scribes to see what they knew. They confirmed that Bethlehem was the place foretold by the prophet. So Herod launched a plan to locate the baby so that he could destroy him! To the wise men he said:

"'Go and search diligently for the child, and when you have found him bring me word, that I too may come and worship him.' When they had heard the king they went on their way; and lo, the star which they had seen in the East went before them, till it came to rest over the place where the child was.

When they saw the child and Mary his mother, they fell down and worshiped him. Then, opening their treasures, they offered him gifts of

gold, frankincense and myrrh. And being warned in a dream not to return to Herod, they departed to their own country by another way" (Mt. 2:8-12).

The gifts the wise men brought were suitable for a king. But Mary and Joseph soon learnt that Jesus was born with a price on his head. Plots were made to kill him: angels had to warn Joseph to escape with Mary and the baby.

"An angel of the Lord appeared to Joseph in a dream and said: 'Rise, take the child and his mother, and flee to Egypt, and remain there till I tell you; for Herod is about to search for the child, to destroy him.' And he rose and took the child and his mother by night, and departed to Egypt, and there remained until the death of Herod. This was to fulfil what the Lord has spoken by the prophet, 'Out of Egypt have I called my son'" (Mt. 2: 13-14).

What does the birth of Jesus mean for us?

- Jesus, truly God and truly human has come down to earth.
- He brings peace, love and true freedom to those who seek him.
- He opens the way to heaven for us.
- He has come to save all people.

What does it teach us?

- God seeks those with an open heart to receive him.
- If you truly seek God, He will find you.
- It's not money, wealth or knowledge that matters because God seeks the lowly and the humble who are looking for Him.
- In revealing himself to the wise men from the East, we know that Jesus has not just come for the Jews but for all of us.

KEY WORDS: Frankincense, Myrrh

1. **QUICK QUIZ:** The Saviour of the world was born in a stable and died with robbers. What evidence can you find for it? Clue: Lk. 23:39-40.

2. **Work in pairs:**
   God can do all things. Why do you think He wanted the birth of Jesus to be like this?

3. **How did the following react to Jesus?**
   - Shepherds
   - Innkeeper
   - King Herod
   - Wise Men

4. "Jesus is the Reason for the Season."
   "Put Christ back into Christmas."
   a) Make a poster for the school using one of the above.
   b) Give a reason for it.
   c) Suggest a way to put it into practice.

5. Those who have no room in their hearts for Jesus are 'spiritually bankrupt'.
   - Explain what is meant by 'bankrupt' and 'spiritually bankrupt'.
   - Give reasons why you agree or disagree with this statement.
   - Give reasons why other people may or may not agree.
   - Try to give examples from scripture to support your opinion.

6. **CHRISTMAS CARDS:** Cards that celebrate the birth of Jesus have almost vanished from the shops and we are happy to buy robins, snowmen, and jingle bells!
   - THINK of what you could do to influence your family and friends to send religious Christmas cards.
   - In pairs: PLAN a course of action.
   - ACT on your plan this week.
   - Write an account of how you got on.

3. The Saviour

Deepen our understanding of the message of John the Baptist. Reflect on the demands it makes on us.

God's Initiative

Throughout the Old Testament, God revealed Himself through Abraham, Moses, the kings and prophets. While the people accepted that they were called to live according to the Law of Moses, they also understood that they would need help from a future Messiah to be their Saviour: one who would save them from their sins and lead them to eternal life with God.

Many of God's Chosen People relied on their own self-sufficiency. They did not acknowledge their need of God and ignored the needs of the poor. But **"God loved the world so much that He gave His only Son, so that everyone who believes in him may not be lost but may have eternal life"** (Jn. 3:16).

Immediately before sending His Son, God chose and sent John the Baptist to **prepare the way – the WAY that JESUS** himself would be.

John the Baptist

John burst in upon the Jewish people, announcing that the coming of the Messiah was imminent. He was preaching in the wilderness of Judea, **"Repent for the kingdom of God is at hand."** He quoted from the prophet Isaiah:
**"The voice of one crying in the wilderness:
Prepare the way of the Lord, make his paths straight."**

"Now John wore a garment of camel hair, and a leather girdle round his waist; and his food was locusts and wild honey. The people went out to him from Jerusalem and all Judaea and the region about the Jordan, and they were baptised by him in the river Jordan, confessing their sins" (Mt. 3:2-6).

For John, an outward show of repentance counted for nothing unless it brought about a lasting change of heart. He warned the Pharisees and Sadducees that they could not say to themselves: "We are children of Abraham so we will be all right". God looks into people's hearts and wants to see if they have faith and trust in Him and are willing to look after those in need of help. The people asked John what they should do to prepare for the coming of the kingdom of God. He answered:

> You tax collectors, don't collect more than is legal.

> You who are rich, you have no need of two coats, give one to the person who has none. You who have food, do the same.

> You soldiers, rob no one by violence or false accusation. Be content with your wages. You must not abuse your position.

> You scribes and Pharisees, who told you that you could escape from the punishment God is about to send? Do those things that will show that you have turned from your sins.

John touched the hearts of many people; they responded to his message and were baptised.

Activities

1. If you had been present with the people, what questions would you have wanted to ask John? In pairs: work out the questions.

2. a) What advice does John the Baptist give to the people to prepare for the coming of God's kingdom?
   b) If John came today, what instructions would he give us to prepare for the kingdom?
   c) In groups, pool your ideas; identify the three most important.
   d) Each group gives suggestions to the teacher for display.

3. a) In groups, plan a 'news broadcast' or 'newspaper headlines' with the message that you believe people need to hear today in order to proclaim the kingdom of God.
   b) Take one message from your group presentation.
      Write an essay on it to show the impact it could have on:
      • your own life;
      • family;
      • friends;
      • the rest of society.

KEY WORDS: repentance, tax collectors

Values

Sometimes the things we value are in stark contrast with the values of the Gospel. The message Jesus has come to give us can only be considered as a bombshell or a revolution.

We know little about the early years of the life of Jesus except that he grew up in Nazareth with Mary and Joseph. Now he commences his public life. His mission is to lead us to the Father. He comes among all sorts of people; many of them are trying to be God's people, to live according to the law. He starts by giving them a new way to live. It is a new beginning: God is going to act through Jesus to turn our values upside down.

Turning Values
Upside Down or Right Way Up

Values A

1. Blessed are the rich and comfortable.

2. Blessed are the bullies.

3. Blessed are those whose every want is satisfied.

4. Blessed are they who get even.

5. Blessed are you when they flatter you and pamper you.

6. Look out for yourself; nobody else will.

7. Avoid pain and suffering at all costs.

8. Success is the name of the game; you are a loser if you don't achieve it.

Values B

1. Blessed are the poor in spirit.

2. Blessed are the meek.

3. Blessed are those who hunger and thirst for righteousness.

4. Blessed are the merciful.

5. Blessed are you when they insult you and persecute you.

6. Give and it will be given to you in good measure.

7. Take up your cross each day and follow me.

8. What profit would it be for you to gain the whole world and suffer the loss of your own soul?

Activities

In groups of four: choose a pair of VALUES.
Two of you represent Values A and two Values B.
Present a mime to show the clash between them.
The rest of the class will have to guess which one it is.

The Beatitudes
(Mt. 5:3-10 adapted)

Jesus taught the people what his values were in the Sermon on the Mount. The first part of this sermon is known as 'The Beatitudes', which means 'blessings'.

Blessed are the poor in spirit,
- those who recognise their need and dependency on God;
- those who admit that they are unable to overcome injustice by their own strength, who listen with open hearts to the word of God;

for theirs is the kingdom of heaven.

Blessed are the meek,
- those who commit themselves to fulfilling God's plan;
- those who share their possessions with the poor;

for they shall inherit the earth.

Blessed are those who mourn,
- those who mourn or suffer because of the prejudices, fears, guilt and pain that separate us from one another;
- those who know they are in need of healing;

for they shall be comforted".

Blessed are the merciful,
- those willing to forgive those who hurt them;
- who show God's care for those in need and build them up with kind words;

for they shall obtain mercy.

Blessed are those who hunger and thirst for righteousness,
- those who are not satisfied until they experience God's life in them;
- those who pray and work for justice;

for they shall be satisfied,

Blessed are the pure in heart,
- those who make time in their busy lives to be aware of the presence of God within them;
- those who strive to live in a way pleasing to God.

for they shall see God.

Blessed are those persecuted for righteousness' sake,
- those who are mocked or persecuted for their belief in God;
- those who are rejected when they put the teaching of God into practice;

for theirs is the kingdom of heaven.

Blessed are the peacemakers,
- those who believe each person is precious in the eyes of God;
- those who detest all forms of bullying and protect others from the bullies;

for they shall be called children of God.

Pause to Reflect

Outside the restaurant,
smells of hot food.
An old man sits, begging.
The people pass by.
Laughter, full appetites, good friendship,
but no one can see his plight or hear his plea.
Lord, have mercy.

> I wonder why people pass by?

Activities

1. **Discuss:** In what ways does the code of behaviour that Jesus gave in the Beatitudes challenge us to think and act differently.

2. **Research:** Where can we see signs of people living the Beatitudes today? Find examples of people who are:
   - rich but use their wealth to build up the kingdom of God;
   - persecuted because he/she is putting the teaching of Jesus into practice;
   - in prison for his/her Christian beliefs;
   - feeding the hungry.

3. **Take one of the Beatitudes.**
   a) Write down one thing you could do to put it into practice this week.
   b) Write a prayer or a reflection about the Beatitude.
   c) Make a classroom display with the title, 'Living the Beatitudes'.

Jesus' Mission

One Sabbath day, Jesus went to the synagogue. He was handed the scroll of the prophet Isaiah and read:

"The Spirit of the Lord is upon me, because He has chosen me to bring good news to the poor.

He has sent me to proclaim liberty to the captives and recovery of sight to the blind; to set free the oppressed and announce that the time has come when the Lord will save His people" (Lk. 4:18-19).

Jesus rolled up the scroll, gave it back to the attendant, and sat down. All the people in the synagogue had their eyes on him, as he said to them, **"This passage of scripture has come true today, as you heard it being read."**

This was the first public sermon that Jesus gave and in it he set out his mission statement: He said he had come for all people, Jews, Gentiles, rich, poor, men and women, disabled and outcast, sinners and righteous.

Jesus was able to say, "Today, this scripture has been fulfilled in your hearing" because he was already working miracles.

Jesus was able to fulfil his mission because he was truly God and, as a man, truly human. "He became truly man while remaining truly God" (Catechism of the Catholic Church para. 464).

KEY WORDS: Sabbath, Gentiles

Those who were suffering from diseases and painful complaints of one kind or another were all brought to him.

Jesus cured
- people with leprosy;
- those paralysed;
- the deaf and dumb.

Jesus
- raised the dead to life;
- converted sinners;
- cast out evil spirits;
- gave sight to the blind.

1. Look at the Power Point presentation of 'Jesus, true God and true man'.

2. a) Your teacher will give you scripture texts which show that Jesus is fully divine and fully human.

   b) Choose one text and explain what it reveals about the nature of Jesus.

   c) Explain how belief in the divinity and humanity of Jesus may inspire and influence you and others.

3. "Jesus is true God and true man, in the unity of his divine person; for this reason he is the one and only mediator between God and man" (Catechism of the Catholic Church para. 464).

   Try to explain how this belief and teaching influences your moral values and behaviour.

   Think about:
   • through Jesus we go to God;
   • your values, actions and possessions.

Jesus' compassion for those who suffer

Let us look in detail at some examples to see how Jesus not only performed the miracles but showed real compassion and insight into the suffering people experienced.

The son of the widow of Nain restored to life

"Now soon afterwards, Jesus went to a town called Nain, accompanied by his disciples and a great number of people. When he was near the gate of the town, it happened that a dead man was being carried out for burial, the only son of his mother, and she was a widow. And a considerable number of the townspeople were with her."

We can imagine that Jesus knew that the mother's heart was broken. She watched her son suffer and prayed to God for help and strength. Her husband had died and now her son. She was all alone. She had no one left, no one to care for her. She had such high hopes and great expectations for her only son – now he was dead. She was comforted by all the people who turned out for the funeral, but realised she would return to an empty house, probably with little or no source of income. Jesus saw a humble person with an open heart crying out to God for help and responded to her needs.

KEY WORDS: divinity, mediator

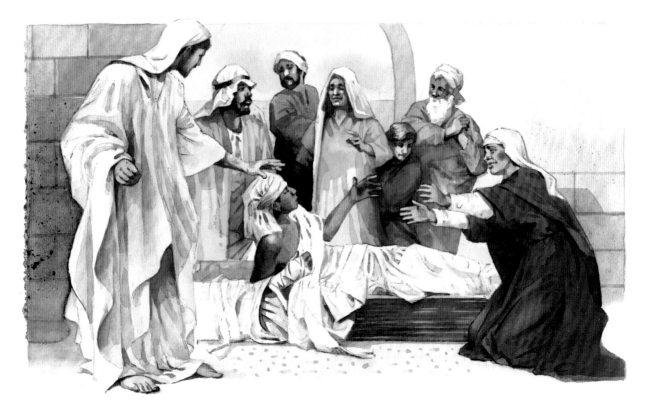

"When the Lord saw her he felt sorry for her. **'Do not cry,'** he said. Then he went up and put his hand on the coffin and the bearers stood still, and he said, **'Young man, I tell you to get up.'** And the dead man sat up and began to talk, and Jesus gave him to his mother. Everyone was filled with awe and praised God" (Lk. 7:11-16).

Pause to Reflect

That night, the widow reflected with her son.
Imagine the conversation.
Think of some of the questions they might have asked each other about this man, Jesus.

Cure of woman with a haemorrhage

"One day, when Jesus was welcomed by a large crowd of people, there was a woman who was suffering from a haemorrhage for twelve years whom no one had been able to cure. She came behind Jesus and touched the fringe of his cloak; and the haemorrhage stopped at that instant. Jesus said, **'Who touched me?'** When they all denied that they had, Peter and his companions said, 'Master, it is the crowds round you, pushing.' But Jesus said, **'Somebody touched me. I felt that power had gone out from me.'** Seeing herself discovered, the woman came forward trembling, and falling at his feet explained in front of all the people why she had touched him and how she had been cured at that very moment. **'My daughter,'** he said, **'your faith has restored you to health; go in peace'** " (Mk. 5:21-34).

KEY WORD: **haemorrhage**

Pause to Reflect

- Try to become very still and imagine you are the neighbour of the woman with the haemorrhage.
- Think of the length of time she has been ill, getting no medical help and how helpless you have felt.
- Her one hope was to meet Jesus, but would she ever get near him with the crowds.
- Imagine how she longed to meet Jesus and hoped in his healing power.
- She finds herself near to Jesus. Her faith overcomes her fear!

Activities

1. Write a report for your Parish Newsletter to describe what happened to the woman with the haemorrhage with the title:
   'God's Power in Human Weakness'.
   Think of the following:
   - What was it about her that Jesus would have felt most of all?
   - How was the woman rewarded?
   Give two examples.

2. a) Work in groups
   - Each person in the group takes a scripture text from the box and studies it.
   - Share what Jesus did and why you think he did it.
   b) On your own write a poem or reflection which compares and contrasts the attitude of Jesus towards the neglected and outcasts with people who tend to neglect and reject the less fortunate today.

   John 5:1-9
   John 4:4-42
   Luke 7:1-10
   Luke 15:4-6
   Luke 17:12-20
   Luke 19:1-10
   Luke 23:34
   Luke 23:43

3. Research
   Find out how Jesus is working through groups and individuals today to bring ALL PEOPLE close to God.
   a) Work in pairs or groups to make a collage to show different aspects of their work.
   b) Put a picture of Jesus in the middle of your collage.
   c) Find out about the work of: The Passage, HCPT, Jubilee Action, SVP, CAFOD, Tearfund, Salvation Army.
   d) For additional charities put into Google: RE: Quest Action – Christian Charities at work.
   e) Remember to include inspirational people you know who make the extra effort to love and help others in need.

Jesus and the Jews

Jesus was born into a Jewish family. When he was twelve years old he became a bar mitzvah which meant that he was a 'son of the Ten Commandments'. He attended synagogue and like all Jewish boys of his age would have been called up to read from the Torah.

Even though Jesus had grown up following all the Jewish religious traditions, he believed he had a special mission to transform Judaism. He would do this in ways that would amaze, challenge, shock, scandalise and infuriate people depending on who they were, what they believed and what they expected of others

There are several incidents of conflict in the gospels between Jesus and some of the Jews. This was because he was not the kind of Messiah they had thought of; they wanted a political type of Messiah to save the righteous Chosen People – they didn't expect one to criticise them. They certainly didn't expect him to reach out to sinners and those who were not born into the Jewish faith.

Jesus' disciples picked corn on the Sabbath

"One Sabbath Jesus was going through the grainfields; and as they made their way his disciples began to pick ears of grain. And the Pharisees said to him, 'Look, why are they doing what is not lawful on the Sabbath?' And Jesus said to them, **'Have you never read what David did, when he was in need and was**

hungry, he and those who were with him: how he entered the house of God, when Abiathar was high priest, and ate the bread of the Presence, which it is not lawful for any but the priests to eat, and also gave it to those who were with him?' And he said to them, 'The Sabbath was made for man, not man for the Sabbath; so the Son of man is lord even of the Sabbath'" (Mk. 2:23-28).

KEY WORDS: Torah, traditions, bread of Presence

1. Why did the Pharisees criticise the disciples for picking corn on the Sabbath?

2. What do you think Jesus meant when he said, "The Sabbath was made for man, not man for the Sabbath"?

3. a) In what ways is the Sabbath intended to help us?
   b) How does it help you?

The woman caught in adultery

One morning, when Jesus came to the temple the scribes and the Pharisees brought a woman who had been caught in adultery, and placing her in the midst they said to him:

Master, this woman was caught in the very act of committing adultery, and Moses has ordered us in the Law to condemn women like this to death by stoning. What have you to say?

They asked him this as a test, looking for something to use against him. "But Jesus bent down and started writing on the ground with his finger. And as they persisted with their question, he looked up and said, '**If there is one of you who has not sinned, let him be the first to throw a stone at her.**' Then he bent down and wrote on the ground again. When they heard this they went away one by one, beginning with the eldest, until Jesus was left alone with the woman, who remained standing here. He looked up and said, '**Woman, where are they? Has no one condemned you?**' 'No one, sir,' she replied. '**Neither do I condemn you,**' said Jesus, '**go away and don't sin any more**'" (Jn. 8:3-11).

Key Point to Remember

- The Scribes and Pharisees wished to condemn; Jesus wished to forgive.
- They used their power to accuse; Jesus used his to understand human weakness.
- They made a public show of the woman's sinfulness; Jesus offers her the possibility of a new life.

KEY WORD: adultery

1. The scribes and Pharisees were out to trick Jesus.
    a) If Jesus had agreed with them that the woman should be punished what do you think they would have said?
    b) If Jesus had said she must not be punished what do you think they would have said?

2. a) What do you think the woman did afterwards?
    b) Think about how this experience may have influenced or inspired her.

3. Explain how the following scripture texts give evidence that Jesus came for all people:
    •   Raising to life of the widow's son;
    •   Cure of the Woman with the haemorrhage;
    •   The woman caught in adultery

    Present your evidence in the form of a front page article in the **GALILEE GAZETTE.**

Dining with the Pharisee

"A Pharisee asked Jesus to dine with him; so he went in and sat at table. The Pharisee was astonished to see that Jesus did not first wash before dinner. And the Lord said to him, **'Now you Pharisees cleanse the outside of cup and plate, while inside yourselves you are filled with extortion and wickedness. You fools! Did not He who made the outside make the inside also? Instead give alms from what you have and then indeed everything will be clean for you'"** (Lk. 11:37-41).

The Jewish law stated that before eating a man must wash his hands in a certain way and that he must also wash them between courses. If Pharisees omitted the slightest

KEY WORD: extortion

detail of this, it was considered a sin. Jesus was quite outspoken when he saw how astonished his host was because he did not wash and said that if Pharisees were as particular about cleansing their hearts as they were about washing their hands they would be better people!

Jesus had little time for those preoccupied with outward appearances and in their hearts judged others. He brought healing and hope to many people who were treated as outcasts. His example and teaching challenges us to help those in need.

Activities

1. PRIVATE EYE
You are a private investigator who has been hired by the Sanhedrin (Jewish Council) to watch Jesus and his work. You have been asked to build up a portfolio of evidence about Jesus' work. Report your findings both positive and negative on Jesus.

2. a) What were the main reasons for Jesus coming into conflict with the religious leaders?
   b) Using the passages you have studied, explain:
      • what Jesus thought the religious leaders were getting wrong or misunderstanding;
      • how he corrected them or pointed out their mistakes;
      • what you think was the most important message Jesus gave.

3. a) How might Christians today learn from Jesus' example and put his teachings into practice in the things that they do and say? For example,
      • moral behaviour;
      • spiritual life.
   b) Explain how Jesus' example and teachings affect your life.

4. RESEARCH: http://www.bbc.co.uk/religion/religions/judaism
   a) Read about the Sabbath.
   b) What could we learn from the Jews about the way they observe the Sabbath that would help us.

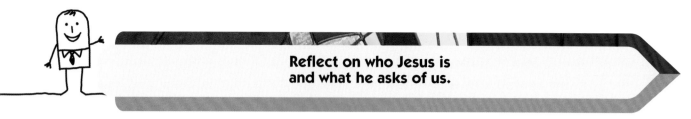

The Big Question

For many of us, the question of who Jesus is for us will shape and determine much of what we do and how we live. We can listen to others teach about him and read many books on his life but it's only **when we allow him into our lives that we will discover him.**

Jesus wants to be with us:

"If we let Jesus into our lives, we lose nothing, nothing, absolutely nothing of what makes life free, beautiful and great. No! Only in this friendship are the doors of life opened wide. Only in this friendship is the great potential of human existence truly revealed. Only in this friendship do we experience beauty and liberation." Pope Benedict XVI

Jesus says:
"I am the true vine,
I am the vine, you are the branches.
Whoever abides in me, and I in him,
he it is that bears much fruit;
for apart from me you can do
nothing" (Jn. 15:1-5).

When we feel
abandoned, Jesus says:
"Know that I am with
you always; yes, to the
end of time"
(Mt. 28:30).

When we are
worried, Jesus
says:
"Do not let your
hearts be troubled;
believe in God,
believe also in me"
(Jn. 14: 1).

When we need
something,
Jesus says:
"Whatever you
ask in my name,
I will do it ...."
(Jn. 14:14).

If we make the effort to live
what Jesus teaches, he
knows this is a sign that we
love him and says:
"If anyone loves me, he will
keep my word, and my
Father will love him, and we
will come to him and make
our home with him"
(Jn.14:23).

When we feel upset, he says:
"Peace I leave with you; my peace
I give to you; not as the world
gives do I give to you. Let not
your hearts be troubled, neither
let them be afraid" (Jn. 14:27).

Choose one of the above quotations.
Write down what you find most helpful about it and say why you chose it.

Activities

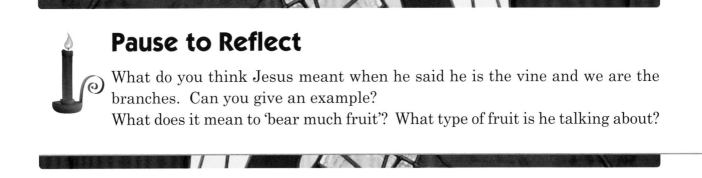

Pause to Reflect

What do you think Jesus meant when he said he is the vine and we are the branches. Can you give an example?

What does it mean to 'bear much fruit'? What type of fruit is he talking about?

Challenges

When we have difficulties and make an extra effort to cope with them, we become more like Jesus and we grow in our relationship with him. Jesus wants us to be co-workers with him so that we can help to transform relationships when they go wrong.

Jesus teaches us:

"Love your enemies" (Lk. 6:27).	"You must love your neighbour as yourself" (Mk. 12:31).	"Do good to those who hate you..." (Lk. 6:27).	"Judge not and you shall not be judged" (Lk. 6:37).

Example:

Jimmy Mizen was a 16 year old boy who was beaten to death, although he refused to fight. He was killed with a shard of glass. It happened in a baker's shop in London on 10th May 2008.

Mrs. Mizen quickly pardoned the person who killed her son. She said, "There is too much anger in the world ... it was anger that killed my son ... if I am angry then I am going to be doing exactly the same as this young chap".

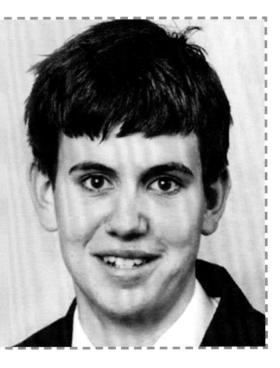

When St. Francis of Assisi encountered challenges he wrote this prayer:

"Lord, make me an instrument
of your peace,
where there is hatred,
let me sow love;
where there is injury, pardon;
where there is doubt, faith;
where there is despair, hope;
where there is darkness, light;
and where there is sadness, joy."

Activities

1. Work in pairs.
   a) List the challenges you encounter at school.
   b) Choose the most difficult one.
   c) What do you think Jesus would advise you to do about it?
   d) Where or how do you think you would get the strength to follow this advice?

2. Think of the challenges that frequently come your way. Write a prayer to ask Jesus to help you cope with them.

Reflect on some people who lived for Jesus.

In God We Trust

When we read the lives of the saints, we allow our minds to be filled with rays of light and life, sometimes to be challenged and always to be uplifted. We are taken beyond our daily experiences to discover how God works in the hearts and minds of those who seek him and open their hearts to him. What follows are a few glimpses of these realities.

St. John Vianney Curé d'Ars
(1786 – 1859)

John Vianney was born in France. He was not considered a bright student at school. It was because of the goodness of his life, rooted in his love for Jesus, that he was accepted for ordination to the priesthood.

After ordination he was sent to a remote and insignificant parish. He believed that he was responding to Jesus' command to 'love one another' and he wanted to do this every hour of the day. It was said that he never seemed to sleep. He spent his days visiting parishioners, celebrating the sacraments and much of the time with Jesus present in the Blessed Sacrament in the church.

Before long, he became known for his extraordinary gifts when hearing people's confession. He was able to unlock the barriers which were keeping some people from knowing and loving Jesus. Word spread and crowds arrived to go to confession. He would be in his little cramped confessional for twelve to eighteen hours a day. In winter, he would shiver with the cold and in summer, suffer in the stifling heat. All the time, he knew Jesus was with him and that was everything he needed.

When asked what he did when he sat in front of the Blessed Sacrament, he replied, 'I look at Him and HE looks at me'.

Towards the end of his life, the railway had to provide special trains to accommodate the hundreds of people who wanted to go to confession to the famous priest, the Curé of Ars. By the time he died in 1859, thousands of people had come to know the love of Jesus through him and he had become one of the most loved people in France.

Activities

1. a) **What type of person was St. John Vianney? Write one sentence to describe him.**
   b) **In groups share your sentence. Sum up what each person says and write one sentence from the group.**
   c) **Make a classroom display of the sentences from each group with a picture of St. John Vianney.**

2. **Why do you think so many people wanted to go to confession to Fr. John Vianney and then give at least four reasons.**

St. Teresa of Avila (1515 – 1582)

Teresa had a dynamic and forceful personality. She was the last person anyone would have expected to become a nun, yet she became one of the most famous nuns of all time. She made her religious profession at a Carmelite Convent when she was nineteen years old.

Teresa was disappointed that being a nun was not as easy and peaceful as she had expected. She found it hard to pray. There were many distractions. Even when she tried, she found it hard to concentrate. Since she liked having friends and being among people, it was difficult to spend time in prayer.
Finally, after many trials, and years of trying, Teresa received the grace she prayed for: God became her best friend. She wanted to spend all her time with Him. She found the peace and happiness she had been looking for with God in her heart.

Her trust in God was so great that, when asked how she intended to open a monastery with only a handful of ducats (coins) in her purse, she answered: 'Teresa and this money are indeed nothing; but God, Teresa and these ducats suffice.'

From her experience, St. Teresa advises us:

"Let nothing upset you,
let nothing startle you.
All things pass,
God does not change.
Patience wins
all it seeks.
Whoever has God
lacks nothing:
God alone is enough."

Many times she had to endure sickness, hunger and poverty. A particular suffering was the misery and hazards of travel at a time when donkey carts were the standard mode of transportation. One time her cart overturned, throwing her into a muddy river. When she complained to God about this ordeal, she heard a voice from within her say, 'This is how I treat my friends.' 'Yes, my Lord,' she answered, 'and that is why you have so few of them.'

She died after having a vision of Jesus and many saints waiting to welcome her into our Heavenly home.

KEY WORDS: nun, Carmelite Convent, monastery

1. 'Whoever has God lacks nothing, God alone is enough'.
   a) What do you think St. Teresa meant by this?
   b) Give your own opinion.
   c) Explain why others might not agree with you.

2. What do you find most interesting about the life of St. Teresa of Avila?
   What can we learn from her?

Fr. Pedro Arrupe S.J. (1907-1991)

Fr. Arrupe was born in Spain in 1907. He was studying medicine at the University of Madrid when he felt God calling him to join the Society of Jesus (Jesuits). He was later sent as a missionary to Japan where he spent twenty-seven years.

He was novice master when Hiroshima was hit by the atomic bomb. With the help of his novices, he turned the novitiate into a hospital. What he witnessed at that time had a profound effect on him. Later, when he became the Superior General of the Society, he wanted all the members to work to alleviate (lessen) the sources of oppression and violence everywhere in the world.

Above all he wanted to share with everyone his profound love of God.

"Nothing is more practical than finding God; that is falling in love in a quiet, absolute, final way with God.
What you are in love with, what seizes your imagination, will affect everything. It will decide what will get you out of bed in the morning, what you will do with your evenings, how you spend your weekends, what you read, whom you know, what breaks your heart, and what amazes you with joy and gratitude.
FALL IN LOVE, STAY IN LOVE.
IT WILL DECIDE EVERYTHING!!!"

KEY WORDS: novices, novitiate

Later on, Fr. Arrupe suffered a terrible stroke which left him paralysed for the last ten years of his life. Just before he lost the power of speech he said:

"More than ever, I find myself in the hands of God.
This is what I have wanted all my life from my youth.
But now there is a difference; the initiative is entirely with God.
It is indeed a profound spiritual experience to know and feel myself so totally in God's hands."

Pause to Reflect

What do you think are the most significant changes that took place in the life of Fr. Arrupe?
What was the most important of all?

Mother Teresa of Calcutta (1910-1997)

"Nowhere on earth are you more welcome. Nowhere on earth are you more loved than by Jesus living and truly present in the most Blessed Sacrament. The time you spend with Jesus in the Blessed Sacrament is the best time you will spend on earth."
"Jesus is the Word made Flesh. The Bread of Life, the Sacrifice offered at Holy Mass for the sins of the world and mine." Mother Teresa did not always feel great inner peace and joy in praying but she always held on in faith.

Who is Jesus for me?

To me, Jesus is my God.
Jesus is my spouse.
Jesus is my life.
Jesus is my love.
Jesus is my all in all.

Mother Teresa believed firmly in the words of Jesus, **"Truly, I say to you, as you did to one of the least of these my brethren, you did it to me"** (Mt. 25:40).
However she firmly believed that without the friendship of Jesus, she could never have persevered in her life of service. No matter how busy or tired she was she would always spend time alone with Jesus every day.

Helping others

For Mother Teresa, Jesus is:
the leper – to wash his hands;
the drunkard – to listen to him;
the (mental) patient – to protect him;
the little one – to embrace him;
the blind – to lead him;
the dumb – to speak to him;
the crippled – to walk with him;
the prostitute – to be removed from danger
and befriended;
the prisoner – to be visited;
the old – to be served. (Meditations)

Mother Teresa firmly believed that while most of
us are not called to be full-time missionaries,
every Christian is a full-time disciple called to
make Jesus present to those around them and to
help to bring God's kingdom on earth. Through the Sacrament of Baptism we have been
commissioned to give witness to Jesus in our daily lives. She said:
"I pray very, very specially for each one of you that we together fulfil God's will in all
things so that we can all look up and see only Jesus in the work that He has entrusted to
us and, that the people can look up and see only Jesus in us."

Activities

1. **Choose a saint or other inspirational person. What was it that inspired
    or motivated this person?**
    *   **What contribution did he/she make to the lives of others?**
    *   **Why do you think this person has been or will be canonized a saint?**
    *   **How might this person influence you or others?**

2. **Create a hymn/song or make a poster using the sayings of one the people
    in this section.**

3. **Show how religious beliefs and teaching have influenced the moral values and
    behaviour of a person you know or heard about. For example, think of somebody
    who worked for justice and peace.**
    *   **Mention the beliefs and teachings this person valued.**
    *   **What actions were taken? What were the results?**

KEY WORD: missionary

Jesus bids Farewell

For forty days after rising from the dead, Jesus stayed on earth and frequently came to see his chosen disciples to prepare them for the time to come when he would no longer be with them.

One evening, the disciples were in the Upper Room with the door locked because they feared the Jews. "Jesus came and stood among them and said to them, **'Peace be with you.'** When he had said this, he showed them his hands and his side. The disciples were glad when they saw the Lord. Jesus said to them again, **'Peace be with you. As the Father has sent me, even so I send you.'** And when he had said this, he breathed on them, and said to them, **'Receive the Holy Spirit. If you forgive the sins of any, they are forgiven; if you retain the sins of any, they are retained'** " (Jn. 20:19-23).

Peter is Chosen

Jesus wanted the eleven disciples to be his representatives on earth. He wanted them to form a community with Peter as the leader, but before saying this to Peter, he tested him to see if he was ready!

Jesus and Simon Peter

Jesus said to Peter,
"Simon, son of John, do you love me more than these others do?"
Peter replied, **"Lord, you know I love you."**
Jesus said, **"Feed my lambs."**
Again, Jesus said,
"Simon, son of John, do you love me?"
"Yes, Lord, you know I love you," said Peter.
Jesus said, **"Tend my sheep."**
And again, Jesus said,
"Simon, son of John, do you love me?"
Peter was upset that he asked him a third time and said,
"Lord, you know everything; you know I love you."
Jesus said, **"Feed my sheep"** (Jn. 21:15-17).

Pause to Reflect

Why do you think Jesus asked Peter the same question three times? Think deeply before you answer and try to give more than one reason. (Clue Mk. 14:66-72).

Peter is Chosen as Leader

On an earlier occasion, when Jesus had asked his disciples who they thought he was, it was Peter who spoke up and said, "You are the Christ, the Son of the living God." Jesus knew that it was God who had revealed this to him.

"I tell you, you are Peter and on this rock I will build my church, and the power of death shall not prevail against it. I will give you the keys of the kingdom of heaven and whatever you bind on earth shall be bound in heaven, and whatever you loose on earth shall be loosed in heaven" (Mt. 16:18-19).
So Peter was chosen to be the leader of the new community.

Jesus gives His Mission, Power and Authority

To Peter and the chosen disciples Jesus said,
"All authority in heaven and on earth has been given to me. Go, therefore, make disciples of all nations; baptise them in the name of the Father and of the Son and of the Holy Spirit, and teach them to observe all the commands I gave you. And know that I am with you always; yes to the end of time" (Mt. 28:18-20).

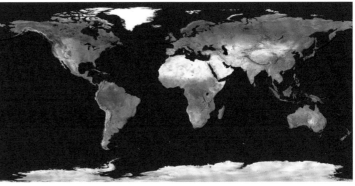

Activities

1. a) **What tasks does Jesus give to his chosen disciples?**
    b) **What words of comfort does Jesus give? Do those words apply to us? How do you know?**

2. **Research Task**
    Use the worksheet that your teacher will give you.
    a) **In box 1 write your own explanation of the Church.**
    b) **Ask six people to explain to you what the Church is.**

    When finished, give the paper to your teacher for use later on.

KEY WORDS: prevail, bind, loose

Scattered... Shattered... Amazed... Astonished ...

Within a period of fifty days, the disciples had seen their Lord and Master crucified, they had fled in fear of their own lives and had just lost all hope when they witnessed the risen Jesus **ALIVE** and with them. They had experienced a whirlwind of astonishing events, one after another and even saw him ascend to heaven. Now they were on their own again.

Pentecost

As instructed by Jesus, the disciples went to the Upper Room in Jerusalem to wait for the Holy Spirit. They were fearful so they locked the door. They remembered Jesus dying on the cross and were afraid they would end up like him. But when Pentecost day came round ....

"Suddenly they heard what sounded like a powerful wind from heaven, the noise of which filled the entire house in which they were sitting; and something appeared to them that seemed like tongues of fire; these separated and came to rest on the head of each of them. They were all filled with the Holy Spirit, and began to speak foreign languages as the Spirit gave them all the gift of speech" (Acts 2: 1-4).

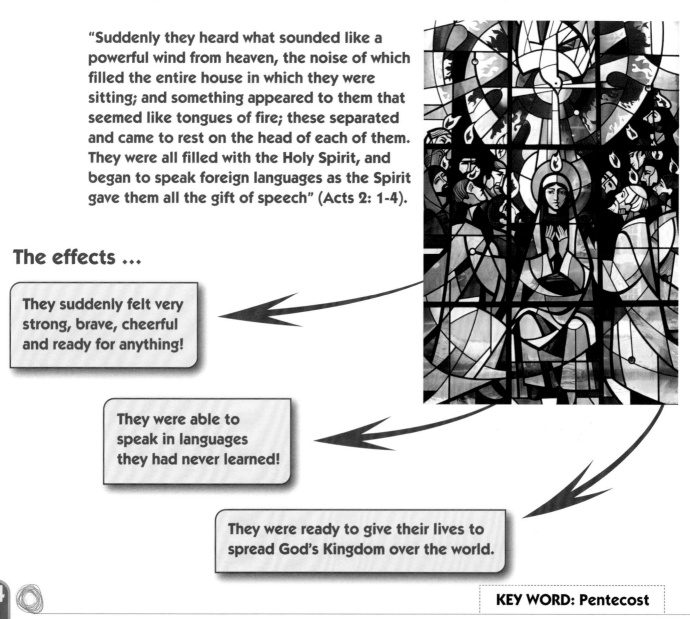

The effects ...

They suddenly felt very strong, brave, cheerful and ready for anything!

They were able to speak in languages they had never learned!

They were ready to give their lives to spread God's Kingdom over the world.

KEY WORD: Pentecost

At the time, there were a great many people in Jerusalem who came from other countries for the Jewish feast of Pentecost which was held every year in memory of the giving of the Law of the Old Testament to Moses. On receiving the Holy Spirit, the apostles came running out into the streets and began to speak about Jesus. All the foreigners were astonished that they understood them in their own language. Of course, there were some sceptics around who said, 'Take no notice, these men are drunk' (Acts 2: 13).

Peter went on to preach the Good News boldly and confidently. He reminded the people of the miracles, wonders and signs which God worked through Jesus and then confronted them with the stark facts.

"This Jesus … you crucified and killed … But God raised him up".

"Repent and be baptised every one of you in the name of Jesus Christ for the forgiveness of your sins; and you shall receive the gift of the Holy Spirit" (Acts 2:23,38).

What Peter and the other apostles said impressed the crowds so much that three thousand people were converted that first day. And that was only the beginning.

Activities

1. In groups, plan a script and act out the events of Pentecost. Show how the coming of the Holy Spirit transformed you from a group of quivering wrecks to people who are willing to risk your lives for the truth.

2. a) Research a variety of illustrations of Pentecost and reflect on them.
   b) Draw your own illustration of Pentecost.
   c) Explain the symbols you have used and the reason for them.

Birth of the Church

The outpouring of the Holy Spirit on the apostles at Pentecost about 30 AD marked the birth of the Church. The twelve apostles were the first members of the Church because they had been the companions of Jesus. They heard all his teaching. They were witnesses of his miracles and his resurrection. Matthias was chosen to fill the place of Judas. Peter, as head of this Christian community, made decisions and governed the infant Church acting with the other apostles. They met together to study, pray and break bread. All who saw them were filled with awe. They knew God was with them.

Read about the early Christian Community Acts 2:42-47 and make a 'Bubble Map' to show six things about the way they lived.

Activities

God works through the Apostles

One day, when Peter and John were going to the temple at the hour of prayer a man who was lame from birth looked at Peter and John expecting to get some money. Peter placed in his hands, not coins, but new life from God.
First, the man clasps Peter's hand.
Then, he is pulled shakily to his feet.
Next, he takes a few wobbly steps.
Finally, he runs and jumps up and down like an excited child praising God.
He cannot contain himself.
No longer is he condemned to sit and beg.
(Acts 3:1-7 adapted)

The lame man ends by thanking God for refusing him what he fervently prayed for and giving him something far greater. The power that was in Jesus was now present and active in his apostles. They had inherited the mission and the authority of Jesus. On the first day, there were over 3,000 converts and the Lord added to their number day by day those who were being saved. Even those who were opposed to the apostles could not deny what was happening and wondered what could be done to get rid of them – within days, numbers had grown to 5,000!

"God's gifts put man's best dreams to shame".
   a) **How does the account of the man who was lame illustrate this?**
   b) **Try to think of an example from your own life or of someone else's.**

Activities

Drama Unfolds

Before returning to his Father in heaven, Jesus had warned the apostles that they would be brought before governors and kings to be tried as enemies for doing his work. They must expect to be imprisoned, beaten and even killed, but just the same, the work would go on and nothing would stop it. He would always be with them, even to the end of the world.

The apostles remembered that Jesus had forewarned them – but they had no idea how quickly events would unfold. Things worked out exactly as Jesus had warned them in the long farewell talk he had with them at the Last Supper (John's Gospel, chapters 13-17). Filled with the Holy Spirit, Peter and the other apostles preached openly and confidently about the Resurrection of Jesus. They worked many miracles among the people, who flocked to listen to them.

"So many signs and wonders were worked by the apostles that the sick were even taken out into the streets and laid on beds and sleeping-mats in the hope that at least the shadow of Peter might fall across some of them as he went past" (Acts 5:15).

Apostles arrested

The excitement generated by such cures was exactly what the Jewish authorities feared. The high priest was jealous. With the backing of the Sadducees they had the apostles put in prison. God was with the apostles: **"At night, an angel of the Lord opened the prison gates and said as he led them out, 'Go and stand in the Temple, and tell all the people about the new Life'"** (Acts 5:19-21).

Stoning of Stephen

As the number of disciples steadily increased, the apostles elected Stephen, a man of great faith, to help them. Stephen was filled with grace and power and began to work miracles and great signs among the people

Before long, he was arrested and brought before the Sanhedrin, the high council. In a powerful speech he showed how the Old Testament prophecies had been fulfilled in Jesus.

He ended by attacking the emptiness of the Temple worship and the blindness of the religious authorities of Jerusalem:

"You stubborn people, with your pagan hearts and pagan ears. You are always resisting the Holy Spirit, just as your ancestors used to do" (Acts 7: 51).

The members of the council were raging and took what he said as blasphemy. They dragged him outside the city and stoned him. Stephen was praying all the time and when the great stones began to strike him, he went on his knees and cried aloud, "Lord, do not count this sin against them!"

An onlooker named Saul approved of the murder. But God had other plans for him!

Activities

1. **Stephen was on his own, no one had taken his side. He could have apologised and taken back what he had said.**
   What would you have done if you were in his situation and why?

2. **a) Read Stephen's Speech which your teacher will give you.**
   b) Pick out four of the most important events that Stephen has mentioned in his speech.
   c) Place them on a timeline.

KEY WORDS: Sadducees, ancestors, blasphemy, Sanhedrin

Saul's Experience

Saul planned to go on persecuting the first Christians until there were none left anywhere. He heard there were many in Damascus, a city about 150 miles from Jerusalem. He set out on his journey determined that no one should stand in his way. Just before he reached the city, suddenly and without warning, a great light, much stronger than the sun, shone around him. He fell down on the ground and heard a voice say, "Saul, Saul, why do you persecute me?" "Who are you, Lord?" he asked, and the voice answered, "I am Jesus, and you are persecuting me. Get up and go into the city and you will be told what you have to do." Saul was soon to understand that persecuting the Christians was the same as persecuting Jesus.

Saul experienced a deep conversion. (You can read

about it in Acts 9:1-19). He began to preach **for** and not **against** Jesus. He showed the Jews that Jesus was really risen from the dead and had sent his Spirit to be with all who believed in him. No matter what happened he wouldn't stop preaching; his arguments were convincing and everyone was listening to him. At last, the Jewish authorities could bear it no longer, so they made a plot to kill him. News of it reached Saul.

Damascus was a city with very high walls. The gates were guarded day and night, but when it was dark the disciples took Saul and let him down from the top of the wall, lowering him in a basket (Acts 9:20-25). It was around this time that Saul's name was changed to Paul.

Activities

a) **What lesson did Jesus teach Saul on the road to Damascus?**
b) **How does that lesson apply to us today?**
c) **Design a logo to help you remember this lesson.**

Peter's Arrest

"It was about the time when King Herod started persecuting certain members of the Church. He beheaded James, the brother of John, and when he saw how that pleased the Jews he decided to arrest Peter as well." This time, he made certain that there would be no escaping and ordered twelve soldiers to guard him. Nevertheless, in the middle of the night, when Peter and two of the soldiers chained to him were asleep and another two standing guard at the door, an angel appeared in the prison cell. Peter tells what happened.

> There I was, chained between two guards but fell asleep nevertheless.
> Suddenly, someone tapped on my shoulder. "Get up!" he said. "Hurry!" The chains just fell from me. Before my very eyes the cell door opened. Stunned, I quickly followed the angel, not knowing where he was leading me. We passed two lots of guards – strange, they didn't seem to see us.
> Next thing, there I was outside the big iron gate all alone, but free. (Acts 12:1-19 adapted)

Much more could be told about the apostles, particularly Peter and Paul. Writing in his second letter to the Corinthians Paul said:

"We are afflicted in every way, but not crushed; perplexed, but not driven to despair; persecuted, but not forsaken; struck down, but not destroyed" (2 Cor. 4:8-9).

In spite of all their sufferings, they experienced a profound joy in knowing that Jesus was with them and they were doing his work.

Activities

Peter went immediately to tell his friends
   a) How do you think Peter's story might have helped them?
   b) Explain how it might help you or other people today. Give examples.

Nero's Persecution

In 64 AD, during the reign of the Emperor Nero, there was a great fire which destroyed a large area of Rome. The Emperor used the Christians as a scapegoat, blaming them for the fire. He had many of them brutally killed. Details of their death are too horrific to describe.

About this time, Peter was in Rome preaching to the new Christians. A famous legend is that the Christians in Rome persuaded Peter, their leader, to flee from Nero's persecutions. As he travelled south from the city along the Appian Way, Peter met Jesus coming the other way.

'Quo vadis Domine? Where are you going, Lord?' Peter asked.
'I am going to Rome to be crucified a second time,' replied Jesus.
At this Peter realised that he could not run away from his mission, so he turned around willingly to accept whatever cross was to come to him.

Tradition also has it that Peter did not consider himself worthy to die in the same way as Jesus, so he asked to be crucified upside down.

Activities

1. **INQUIRY BRIEF** – Work in pairs: one of you takes the part of Paul and the other is a lawyer appointed by the Roman Governor to cross-examine him. The evidence base for both of you is the account given in Acts 22. You must study this and make notes before the inquiry starts.

2. Look back at the prophecies of Jesus made on page 67. How have the prophecies been fulfilled in the stories you have read?

3. Imagine you are one of the twelve apostles. A number of years have passed since that first Pentecost and you have been looking back on your life. You are amazed at how things have turned out. You decide you need to write down some of these memories.
   a) Write a short chapter on the dramatic events that took place in your life.
   b) Explain how your experiences affected your life in the years after Pentecost.

KEY WORD: scapegoat

The People of God are the Church

God took the initiative to bring scattered people together and chose Moses to lead them out of slavery in Egypt to be his very own people.

Do you remember when God spoke to Moses on Mount Sinai? God made a covenant with Moses and the people. He wanted them to be His Chosen People. He promised to be their God and in return asked them to be His people:

"If you will obey My voice and keep My covenant, you shall be My own possession among all peoples" (Ex. 19:4-6).

Now Jesus has come for us. In and through Jesus, God has made a new Covenant with us.

In this new Covenant Jesus handed over himself in love to the Father for us. He died on the Cross for us. So for us to fulfil our part of the covenant, we have to hand over ourselves to God.

St. Peter tells us: "Once you were no people but now you are God's people. Once you had not received mercy but now you have received mercy".

WHO ARE WE?

We are the Church. We are a people whom God called "out of darkness into his wonderful light". The light we live in is the knowledge that we have been chosen, loved and owned by Jesus. Jesus has given us our new identity. Why ? So "that we may declare the wonderful deeds of God" (1 Pet. 2:9-10).

As Members of the Church - what do we have to do?

The challenge each day for each one of us is to hand over our lives to God and with God's help, to one another. This means that our lives have to focus on how we can love and help one another. Instead of thinking all the time of what we want for ourselves, we find ways of putting the needs of others first.

God can work wonders through us when we hand over our lives to Him: **LET GO, LET GOD!** When our lives are centred on God they take on a new meaning and purpose. God has given us our identity so that **HIS** identity might shine through us!

Activities

1. a) Explain in your own words what Jesus has done for us.
    b) Why has he done this?
    c) What can we do in return?

2. • Imagine you are either Peter or Paul and you are looking back on your life.
    • How did you hand over your life to Jesus?
    • With the gift of His Spirit, how did you help others?
    • What did it cost you?
    • Was it worth it? Why? Why not?
    • What advice would you give to young people preparing for their future?

3. God has given us our identity so that HIS identity might shine through us. Give examples to explain what this means.

4. Work in groups.
    a) Re-read the text above on what we have to do as the People of God, the Church.
    b) List all that staff and students in your school do which show that they are the People of God, the Church; don't just choose the obvious things.
    c) On your own, design a webpage 'Witnesses Today' illustrating two or three things you and others do. It can be a personal experience of what you did for another person or someone did for you in school.
    d) Explain the influence this had on your life and the lives of others.

5. Research: Look at the Young Christian Workers' website.
    a) What is the YCW?
    b) What is their vision and mission?
    c) What is 'Impact'?
    d) What does 'Impact' do for young people?
    e) In what ways do you think YCW helps young people to live as members of the Church?
    f) What do you think is the meaning of their logo 'The difference is you'?

YCW
The Difference Is You

The Church: The Body of Christ

Pause to Reflect

- If we are the People of God that make the Church, then what is it that will draw us together?

- What or who will give us the strength to build a strong community of faith?

- Who will give us the courage to love others so that all will know that we are the disciples of Jesus?

The EUCHARIST makes us CHURCH
The Church cannot be Church, cannot live, exist or survive without the Eucharist.

St. Paul tells us that, at the Last Supper Jesus had with his apostles before he died, he took bread, and when he had given thanks, he broke it and said, **"This is my body which is handed over for you. Do this in remembrance of me"** (1 Cor. 11: 23-24). We know that the following day, Good Friday, Jesus freely offered his life on the Cross for us.

When Jesus said **"Do this in remembrance of me"**, he meant, **"Hand over yourselves as I handed over myself"**. So, when we hand ourselves over to Jesus, we become deeply united with **HIM** and with each other. We become **"Church"**. We live the mystery of the Church when, with Jesus, we hand over ourselves to him. Then, with his help, we strive to help others.

Your teacher will give you examples of what some people try to do in order to hand over their lives to Jesus. Make a plan of what you could do.

Activities

Handing over: becoming the Body of Christ – the Church

> **What does it mean to hand over our lives?**

> **To hand over our lives to Jesus means to get out of self-interest, self-will and self-pity.**

> **That's tough! How can we do it?**

> **First, we ask Jesus everyday for HIS HELP and with his help we can help others.**

It is natural for us to think of what we want, what we need, what we would like, what we prefer before we think of others. There is a selfish streak in all of us.

How can we tell if we are handing over ourselves to Jesus?

We remember that what we do to one another we do to Jesus.
So instead of thinking just of ME, I think of those with me to see how I can be of help to them.

Instead of just wanting to do my own will – I find out what others would like.

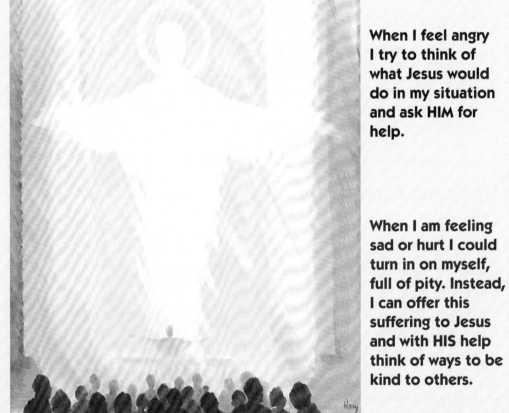

When I feel angry I try to think of what Jesus would do in my situation and ask HIM for help.

When I am feeling sad or hurt I could turn in on myself, full of pity. Instead, I can offer this suffering to Jesus and with HIS help think of ways to be kind to others.

OUR AIM is to HAND OVER to Jesus in our daily life, in our family, in school and with friends. So when we receive the BODY OF CHRIST at Mass, we know that we receive Jesus himself. So we can truly say, AMEN, which means, 'I am committed to being the Body of Christ' – that is THE CHURCH.

It is in the EUCHARIST that Jesus will give us the strength and courage to hand over our lives to loving and serving others so that we are truly HIS BODY – the CHURCH.

Pause to Reflect

In times of persecution, it was the Eucharist that mattered.
Around 200 AD, when Christians were being arrested, tortured and even put to death, they went underground to celebrate the Eucharist so that they could draw strength from it to endure all that lay before them.

In 16th-century England, during the time of Queen Elizabeth I, members of the Catholic Church were being hounded down and priests had to seek refuge in hiding places like dilapidated barns, holes in walls and attics. No matter what happened during these times of persecution, the one thing the people would not give up was the Mass. It was the Mass that mattered. In the Mass, they handed their lives over to Jesus and he gave himself to them. In this way, they drew strength to face whatever lay ahead.

Activities

1. **Watch the Power Point presentation: Priests' hiding holes.**

2. a) **Give reasons why the Eucharist (Mass) was so important in times of persecution.**
   b) **Why do you think it is important today?**

Living the Eucharist today

Today, we are the new People of God, asked to live fully committed lives - handing over self and building up the Body of Christ in order to be CHURCH. So just as the human body counts on each cell to do its part, the Body of Christ counts on each of us to do our part. As St. Paul said, "If one part of the body suffers, all the other parts suffer with it" (1 Cor. 12:26).

We may think that this challenge is far too great for us. We look at our lives and think of the things we do wrong. We see others like ourselves, sinful yet struggling to become what God wants us to be.

It is true the Church is full of sinners and some great sinners! But Jesus exists in the human Church and he is always ready to forgive us when we turn to him for help. We have seen in the many examples of Jesus with sinners that he always accepted them. He didn't approve of their sin or wrongdoing. He said: "Go and sin no more" and he continued to love them.

1. Your teacher will give you back your 'Research Sheet' on the Church.
   a) Read your own explanation of the Church.
   b) Write another explanation – but first, think of all that you have been studying.

2. Study the explanations other people gave of the Church. Choose a way to explain the meaning of the Church that you could pass on to others. It might be a poster, booklet, Power Point presentation or something for the school website.

3. Each time we gather to celebrate the Eucharist we celebrate being Church. At the end of the celebration we are told: Go in peace to love and serve the Lord. On each day this week, take time to reflect upon how you can fulfil this command. Keep a daily diary of your reflections.

4. How far would you agree with the following statement? 'It was easier to become a Christian in AD30 than it is today.' Give reasons for your answers and try to look at things from more than one point of view.

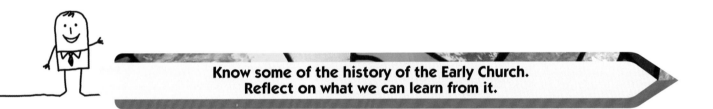

Know some of the history of the Early Church.
Reflect on what we can learn from it.

Spread of Christianity

The rapid spread of Christianity was amazing. By the end of the first century, there were approximately half a million Christians; by the year 200 AD there were two million and by 350 AD there were about ten million.

We may wonder why and how Christianity spread so quickly. One of the reasons for this was that St. Paul completely changed his whole life after Jesus appeared to him on the road to Damascus. Before that, he was a very strong Pharisee bent on persecuting the Christians. But his experience on this road made him realise that he wanted to completely and utterly change. From that moment, he no longer persecuted the Christians but joined them. He took himself off for a few years to reflect on it and then he became the most important missionary in the history of the Church.

Paul writes:
"Five times I was given the thirty-nine lashes by the Jews; three times I was whipped by the Romans; and once I was stoned. I have been in three shipwrecks, and once I spent twenty-four hours in the water. In my many travels I have been in danger from floods and from robbers, in danger from fellow-Jews and from Gentiles; there have been dangers in the cities, dangers in the wilds, dangers on the high seas and dangers from false friends" (2 Cor. 11:24-27).

"I shall be very happy to make my weaknesses my special boast so that the power of Christ may stay over me, and that is why I am quite content with my weaknesses, and with insults, hardships, persecutions, and the agonies I go through for Christ's sake for it is when I am weak that I am strong" (2 Cor. 12:9-10).

However, most of the work of spreading the Good News of Jesus was done by ordinary Christians, people whose everyday work and care for others brought them into contact with people who had not heard the Gospel.

At this time, many people had lost faith in the pagan gods and were looking for something to give meaning to their lives. They no longer trusted their political leaders. Their cruel sports had lost their appeal and they had experienced the emptiness of drunkenness and other sorts of amusements. There were a number of new religious movements from the East attracting attention, but none had the lasting appeal of Christianity. Christianity was based on a real historical person – Jesus Christ. Its message of God's love and forgiveness made a lot of sense to people wanting to lead a good life.

Most of all, it was the example of the young Christian communities living out what they believed, which was clear evidence that this was the true Church. "See how these Christians love one another," people said, and this contrasted with the emptiness of their own lives.

Why did Christianity spread so quickly?
> a. The Romans had built good roads.
> b. Paul was a gifted preacher.
> c. The Spirit of God was at work.
> d. Roman rule brought peace, so it was safe to travel.
> e. The Greek language was common to all so the message could be spread.
> f. People were searching for truth.
> g. Some people were tired of polytheism.
> h. Christianity brought a message of love, forgiveness and hope.
> i. Sea travel was comparatively safe.

From the above list choose the three most important reasons why you believe Christianity spread so quickly. Say why you chose them.

Christians go underground

During the first three centuries Christians lived in fear of their lives. Most of the other religions were accepted probably because it was considered a good idea to have as many gods (polytheism) as possible looking after the people.

At first, the Roman authorities accepted the new Christians. However, when they witnessed the growth of the Christian communities they became suspicious of them. Why? It was because they worshipped only one God (monotheism) and did not consider the Emperor of Rome a god and would not worship him.

In 200 AD, a law was passed that all Roman citizens must have a certificate stating that they had offered sacrifice to the Emperor. For anyone who did not have it, the penalty was death. As a result many Christians were arrested, tortured and put to death.

It was during this time that the Christians used code words and signs as a means of communication. One of the most famous was the Chi Rho, formed from the first two letters of the Greek word for Christ.

As it was no longer safe for the Christians to meet in the city, they took advantage of the law which allowed them to have underground burial places and met there. These meeting places were usually around the crypt of a martyr and were large enough to hold a number of worshippers. They are known as the 'catacombs' which comes from the Greek meaning 'beside the caves'.

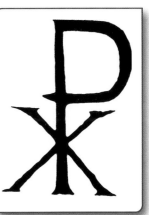

There are several Christian catacombs in Rome which can be visited today, the most famous are St. Calixtus, St. Sebastian, and St. Priscilla.

KEY WORDS: crypt, martyr

Here are some of the symbols that the Early Christians used to communicate with each other:

Alpha and Omega are the first and the last letters of the Greek alphabet. They mean that Jesus Christ is the beginning and the end of all things.

The cross with the anchor means perseverance in bearing with difficulties.

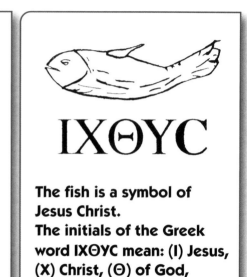

The fish is a symbol of Jesus Christ.
The initials of the Greek word ΙΧΘΥC mean: (I) Jesus, (X) Christ, (Θ) of God, (Y) Son, (C) Saviour.

Constantine's Conversion

While there were many conversions throughout the history of the Church, one of the most notable for the early Church was that of the Roman Emperor, Constantine.

In 312 AD, while preparing his army for battle, he had a very vivid dream. In this dream he saw a cross in the sky and on it were the words, 'In this sign you will conquer'. He understood that he was to put this sign on his soldiers' shields.

Constantine won the battle and believed that the Christians' God had helped him. So after it, he had the CHI RHO sign inscribed on the Imperial banners and the soldiers' shields. He even regarded himself as a Christian even though he was not baptised until he was on his deathbed in 337 AD.

From that time, persecution of Christians by the Romans stopped and they were even given donations of large buildings (basilicas) to use for worship.

In 380 AD, Emperor Theodosius made Christianity the official religion of the Roman Empire and paganism was forbidden. After a short period, the Catholic Church spread throughout Europe and it had a tremendous influence on the lives of all Europeans – on politics, law, morality, family life and education.

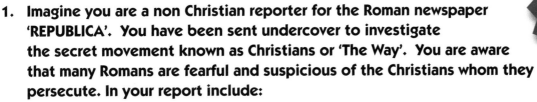

Activities

1. Imagine you are a non Christian reporter for the Roman newspaper 'REPUBLICA'. You have been sent undercover to investigate the secret movement known as Christians or 'The Way'. You are aware that many Romans are fearful and suspicious of the Christians whom they persecute. In your report include:
   • What they believe.
   • What they do and where they meet.
   • Are they to be feared?
   • What gives them courage?
   • You need to evaluate whether Roman fears and suspicions about them are justified.

2. Work in pairs:
   a) List the challenges that the early Christians encountered.
   b) Now list the challenges you face as a Christian today.
   c) What are the causes?
   d) What are the solutions?

3. If Christianity were outlawed in this country today how would this affect:
   • your life?
   • your family?
   • your education?
   • our society?

4. a) Watch the Power Point presentation on the Church in China.
   b) Research the 'Aid to the Church in Need' website.
   c) In approximately how many countries are Christians suffering for their faith?
   d) Choose one country and try to explain why Christians are suffering.
   e) Think of one thing you can to do help this country.

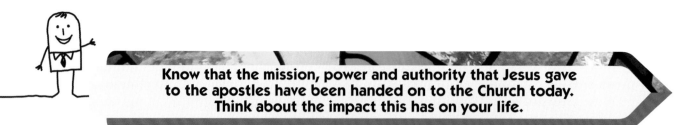

Know that the mission, power and authority that Jesus gave to the apostles have been handed on to the Church today. Think about the impact this has on your life.

The Ordained Ministry of the People of God

We know that every country in the world has to have some form of government for it to function. Today, the Catholic Church has spread all over the world. The word 'catholic' comes from the Greek word meaning 'universal'. It is a world Church. It is much, much larger than even a cluster of countries put together so, of necessity, it has to have a structure or government.

We know Jesus appointed Peter as head of the Church on earth. He became the first Pope and the cardinals, archbishops and bishops are the successors of the apostles.

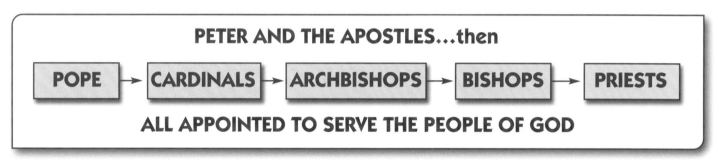

PETER AND THE APOSTLES...then

POPE → CARDINALS → ARCHBISHOPS → BISHOPS → PRIESTS

ALL APPOINTED TO SERVE THE PEOPLE OF GOD

The cardinals elect a new Pope. The archbishops are responsible for very large dioceses known as archdioceses. The bishops are responsible for a local area or 'diocese'. Each diocese is made up of parishes with a parish priest who reports to the bishop.

Mission, Power and Authority passed on ...

Jesus has passed on his mission, power and authority to the apostles (Mt. 28: 16-20). They have passed it on to the Church today. All of us, because we have received the Sacrament of Baptism, have a responsibility to witness to Jesus by the way we live. We have to remember that **WE** are the Church, you and I are the Church. I cannot be a true Christian without being Church and I cannot be Church without the Eucharist.

The Pope, under the guidance of the Holy Spirit, together with the cardinals, archbishops and bishops, guides the Church. They keep the Church free from error in matters of faith and morals.

Youth Club

Mothers & Toddlers Group

Mission Group

School

Together with the priests, they are the ordained ministers of the sacraments and they have to pass on the teaching of the Church and preach the Word of God.

The specific duty of the bishop is to care for all the people in his diocese and to pass on the teaching of the Church to them.

The lay people are all those baptised who are not called by God to the ordained ministry within the Church. They are called in a special way to bring Jesus Christ to the world through a variety of different ministries, such as mothers, fathers, doctors, nurses, teachers, builders, secretaries, chefs, politicians and many other roles.

The Religious Orders are another important part of the Church. They are men and women who have taken vows of poverty, chastity and obedience and have chosen to live their lives as monks, priests, brothers, sisters or nuns. The Religious Orders have spread all over the world; many of them have brought Christianity to the far corners of the earth.

Activities

1. a) **What is the name of the Pope?**
    b) **Which diocese do you live in?**
    c) **Who is your bishop?**
    d) **What is the name of your parish priest?**
    e) **What is the name of your church?**
    f) **What do you know about the name of your church?**

2. **Bring in your parish Newsletter.**
    a) **In pairs, discuss how it reflects the mission of the Church. Are there any activities or groups that are not represented that you think should be there?**
    b) **Take photos of your parish church building.**
    c) **Make a presentation or a poster to explain the key features of the building.**

3. **In Parish Groups: Discuss what you could do to contribute to the life of your parish. Decide on one or two definite things and write as a group to your parish priest to present your proposals to him.**

4. **Work in groups: Your teacher will give you a worksheet.**
    Imagine you are lay missionaries on a very poor island. You have been given 6,000 units to improve the quality of life for the people.
    Think carefully about the spiritual and physical needs of the people. Decide what you will spend your units on and give detailed reasons for your decisions.

5. **Research Project:**
    Research the life of a Religious Order. Make a Power Point presentation or an Information Booklet: explain their mission, work, prayer life and the countries they are in.

5.   The Sacraments

Deepen our understanding of the sacraments. Reflect on how they can help us.

Do you have the answers?

As you grow up, you will be meeting people of different religions and faith groups. Your friends will want to know what you believe and why. It is very important that you have thought through what the Church teaches and can speak with conviction.

During the coming weeks, you will have the opportunity to deepen your understanding of:
- why we need the sacraments;
- what the Church teaches about them;
- what they will do for you.

In particular, we will study the Sacraments of Baptism, Reconciliation as well as the Sacrament of the Sick.

Why do we need the sacraments?

In the beginning, God created man and woman out of love in a relationship of friendship with Him. He gave them the gift of **"freedom"** because He wanted them to *freely* choose to live happily with Him forever.

However, the first man and woman were tempted by the Evil One and they misused their gift of freedom. They turned against God, went their own way and forgot about Him. This first sin was called Original Sin because it was committed at the origin of the human race. We are all affected by it, because we are all members of the human race.

Through this **Original Sin**, we lost the special friendship with God, which was **original grace**. Nothing could ever be the same again until God sent his only Son, Jesus, to save us from our sins and bring us back to eternal life with God.

What is a sacrament?

A sacrament is an encounter or meeting with Jesus Christ and the person who is receiving the sacrament. When a person receives a sacrament they receive God's love, care, courage and understanding – this is what we call God's grace. The celebration of the sacrament is the outward sign.

KEY WORDS: Original Sin, Evil One

Jesus is THE SACRAMENT of God.
Jesus is God.
Jesus makes God visible in the world.
Through Jesus, we meet God in the sacraments.
We receive God's sanctifying grace through the sacraments.

Jesus has passed on his power and authority to the Apostles and their successors, the Pope, bishops and priests.

Jesus strengthened the faith of the Apostles. Through God's grace we are able to strengthen the faith of others.

Jesus forgave sin. Through God's grace we are able to forgive those who hurt us.

Jesus fed the hungry. Through God's grace we can feed the hungry.

Jesus healed the sick. Through God's grace we can cure the sick.

In John's Gospel, Jesus has used the image of the vine and its branches to help us understand how the sacraments keep us close to him and give us grace.

"I am the vine, you are the branches.
Whoever abides in me, and I in him,
he it is that bears much fruit;
for apart from me you can do nothing" (Jn. 15:4-5).

Just as life flows through the vine from the roots out into the branches, so the life of Jesus flows into people receiving the sacraments. Jesus has said:
"I have come that they (we) may have life and have it to the full" (Jn. 10:10).

Pause to Reflect

- Why do you think Jesus said: "apart from me you can do nothing"?
- Where are we going to get the help we need from Jesus?
- Draw or write something that will remind you of the words, "I am the vine".

KEY WORDS: sanctifying grace, abides

The Sacraments

The life of Jesus comes to us in the form of seven sacraments:

In the **SACRAMENT OF BAPTISM** we enter into the life of Jesus and receive his Spirit. We are cleansed of original sin. We become members of the Church and try to be like Jesus by being kind to one another. As in every sacrament, Jesus offers us sanctifying grace to help us on our journey through life.

CONFIRMATION gives us the gifts of the Holy Spirit and we affirm the promises made at our Baptism.

We are given gifts which are not just for ourselves, but for us to use to help others. We are called by God to live more like Jesus and to share in the work of Jesus in our world.

This sacrament gives us the strength and gifts to do what God asks of us in our daily life. But we have to learn to 'tune in' to what God asks of us.

THE EUCHARIST When we receive Holy Communion we receive Jesus truly present in the form of bread and wine. His presence in us helps us to grow in our love of God and gives us the strength to help other people.

MARRIAGE brings the blessing of Jesus. He gives the married couple the help to love one another with God's love.

This love is more than just feeling, it is rooted in commitment and service to each other and to all people.

RECONCILIATION offers inner healing; it is God's plan to heal, renew, transform and strengthen us for everyday living. This sacrament helps us to grow in our love of God.

HOLY ORDERS bring a special grace of the Holy Spirit to help the person who acts in the place of Jesus.

ANOINTING OF THE SICK gives strength, peace and courage to help the person overcome the difficulties that go with serious illness or the frailty of old age.

This grace is a gift of the Holy Spirit to help us renew our faith and trust in God.

1. **Work in pairs.**
   a) Write down the key words or phrases in the section called 'The Sacraments' on the previous page.
   b) Identify similarities and differences between the sacraments.

2. **USE IT or LOSE IT**
   Choose one sacrament. Dramatise or make a flow diagram to show how you can **USE** the gift of this sacrament to live it out or fail to do so and **LOSE IT**.

3. **Effects of the sacraments.** Your teacher will give you this diagram to complete.

What it does for us?	How would it change the way a Christian lives his/her life?

4. a) How can we 'tune in' and be receptive to God coming to us in everyday life?
   b) What might 'block' God coming to us?
   c) Write an action plan to help you strengthen your 'reception' from God.

Living out the sacraments

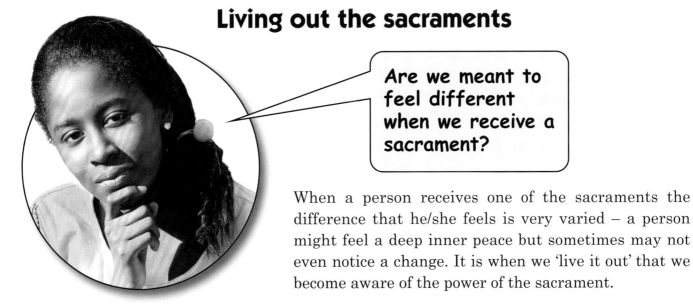

Are we meant to feel different when we receive a sacrament?

When a person receives one of the sacraments the difference that he/she feels is very varied – a person might feel a deep inner peace but sometimes may not even notice a change. It is when we 'live it out' that we become aware of the power of the sacrament.

It is a *little bit like* Paul who received a gift of a very precious violin from his grandfather. He was very pleased to receive the gift but time passed, he never learnt to play and the violin just lay in the corner of his room. This was a gift he never used.

Think about this: each time, we go to the Eucharist (Mass) and receive Jesus in Holy Communion he is really and truly present within us. We do not see him with our physical eyes. Nevertheless, he is truly present. He is offering us his life and love. From this, we will have the grace to know Jesus better and to be kind and helpful to others.

Pause to Reflect

"Christ has no body now on earth but yours.
Yours are the only hands with which he can do his work.
Yours are the only eyes through which his compassion can shine upon a troubled world.
Christ has no body now on earth but yours." St. Teresa of Avila

Activities

a) How can we now be Christ's body on earth as in St. Teresa's prayer?
b) How do the sacraments give us the grace to do this?

Understand what the Sacrament of Baptism is, how it happens and what it does for us.

God's Plan for Us

God's plan for each one of us is that we should be like His Son (Rom. 8:29).
God wants us to develop a deep personal relationship with Jesus. For this to happen we have to be reborn into his life.

Jesus explained this to Nicodemus, a Pharisee and elder of the Jews: a person is born physically of human parents, but is born spiritually of the Spirit:

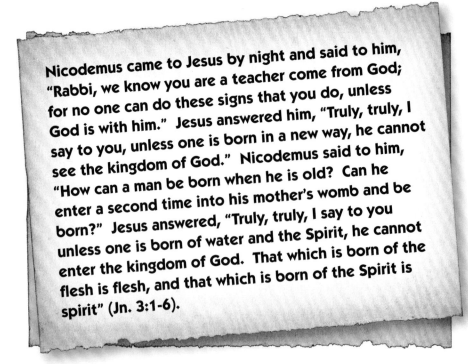

Nicodemus came to Jesus by night and said to him, "Rabbi, we know you are a teacher come from God; for no one can do these signs that you do, unless God is with him." Jesus answered him, "Truly, truly, I say to you, unless one is born in a new way, he cannot see the kingdom of God." Nicodemus said to him, "How can a man be born when he is old? Can he enter a second time into his mother's womb and be born?" Jesus answered, "Truly, truly, I say to you unless one is born of water and the Spirit, he cannot enter the kingdom of God. That which is born of the flesh is flesh, and that which is born of the Spirit is spirit" (Jn. 3:1-6).

1. Some people have difficulty understanding what Jesus said to Nicodemus.
   Discuss in groups, try to explain and give examples of the following:
   a) the kingdom of God;
   b) the difference between physical and spiritual birth.

2. Imagine you are Nicodemus. Write a report for the Pharisees explaining what Jesus believes Baptism does for his followers.

The Sacrament of Baptism

What happens when we are baptised?

When we receive the Sacrament of Baptism, we are 'plunged into' the person of Jesus Christ in mystery. This is a mystery – we are not going to understand fully how it happens but St. Paul says we have 'put on' or are 'clothed in' Christ Jesus in a very personal way (Gal. 3:27). We have entered into the life of Jesus. It is as if we are born again into the very life of God.

Infant Baptism

But how does it happen?

Many parents have their baby baptised soon after the birth. The parents and godparents take on the responsibility for the baptism of the young child. The family must be members of the Church and believe in the Sacrament of Baptism and desire it for their child.

The Baptismal Ceremony

The baptismal ceremony starts at the entrance to the church building. The priest welcomes the child and parents.

'You have asked to have your child baptised. In doing so, you are accepting the responsibility of training him/her in the practice of the faith. It will be your duty to bring him/her up to keep God's Commandments as Jesus Christ taught us, by loving God and our neighbour....'

The priest asks the godparents if they are willing to help the parents to do this. Then the baby is welcomed into the Christian family:

'(Name), the Christian Community welcomes you with great joy. In its name I claim you for Christ our Saviour by the Sign of his Cross. I now trace the sign of the cross on your forehead and invite your parents and godparents to do the same.'

The sign of the cross is a symbol that the baby now belongs to God.

The Word of God

A passage from the Bible is read, for example the text on Nicodemus (Jn. 3:1-6).

Exorcism and Anointing

Jesus gave the apostles power over evil spirits. This power is passed on through the Pope and bishops to priests. In the Sacrament of Baptism, the priest prays:
'O God, you sent your Son to cast out the power of Satan, set this child free from Original Sin.'

The child is freed from the control of all evil forces. However, he or she will still have free will. This means that when the child is old enough to know the difference between right and wrong he/she has the freedom to choose to do good or evil.

The priest anoints the child with the oil of **catechumens** (a catechumen is someone who is preparing to be baptised). The oil is a sign of strength and healing.

Baptismal Promises

The baptismal promises are made by the person who intends to live the Christian life. When a baby is being baptised it is the parents and godparents who make the promises for him/her. These promises include a rejection of all sin and a public statement of Christian beliefs which are found in the Apostles' Creed.

The Baptism

The priest pours water three times over the forehead of the child while saying:
'(Name) I baptise you in the name of the Father and of the Son and of the Holy Spirit.'

The Water

The water is a symbol of new life in the family of God and cleansing from sin.

The Anointing with Chrism

The child is anointed again, but this time with the oil of chrism. It is a symbol of being chosen for a special task in life.

The White Garment

The priest puts a white garment around the child. It is a symbol of new life and faith in Jesus. St. Paul said that the child is 'clothed' in Christ Jesus.

The Baptismal Candle

A candle is given to one of the parents who lights it from the great paschal candle which represents the resurrection of Jesus. It is a reminder to parents that their child is always to walk in the light of Jesus who is the light of the world. The flame is a symbol of life and knowledge.

1. Make a booklet to give to people who are not Christians but will be attending the baptism of a baby. (You may wish to work with a partner and divide the tasks).
   Explain:
   a) what happens during the ceremony;
   b) what the symbols mean;
   c) the role of (i) parents; (ii) godparents;
   d) the meaning of the sacrament.

2. Homework task: Find out everything you can about your own baptism. Interview your parents. Who were your godparents? Who was present? Why did your parents decide to have you baptised?

Adult Baptism

When an adult receives the Sacrament of Baptism this should mark his or her final break with their old lifestyle and the start of a new lifestyle as a disciple of Jesus and a member of the Church.

The Church teaches that a dramatic transformation takes place in the baptised person by the power of the Holy Spirit. The person is cleansed of original sin and all personal sins and is reborn as a child of God. The person receives sanctifying grace which is a share in God's own life. The Sacrament of Baptism imprints an indelible spiritual "mark" on the person. No sin can erase this "seal" of the Spirit which the baptised person carries into eternity. For this reason, the Sacrament of Baptism cannot be repeated (Catechism of the Catholic Church, para. 1272).

From ancient times, the Sacrament of Baptism is received by the catechumen, that is, the person to be baptised, going down into a pool and three times being immersed under the water and three times raised up. This symbolises dying and being born again into the very life of God. However, the form that is more frequently used today is the pouring of water three times over the person's head.

KEY WORDS: Indelible mark

1. a) What are the three things that water symbolises in the Sacrament of Baptism?
   b) Explain each of them.

2. The Sacrament of Baptism imprints an indelible spiritual "mark" on the person.
   a) Explain what this means.
   b) What effect does this have on the person receiving it?

3. You are going to make a Documentary Programme for TV on the Sacrament of Baptism. Work in groups to decide how you are going to present it. Will you:
   • interview people and if so who?
   • act out the Baptism using a 'voice-over' explanation?
   • explain the difference baptism will make to the person?
   Choose a group to video.

Reflect on how Jesus explains God's unconditional love for us.

The Lost Son

We are going to reflect on the parable of the Lost Son as a preparation for exploring the Sacrament of Reconciliation.

Let us imagine we are hearing this parable for the very first time. The Pharisees and scribes had passed judgement on Jesus. They said **"This man cannot be a man of God because he welcomes sinners, mingles and eats with them"** (Lk. 15:2). So it is because of their false ideas about God that Jesus told the parable of the Lost Son.

Pause to Reflect

Before we hear the parable we need to remember that there is a bit of the Pharisee in each one of us. We can all be self-righteous and judge others narrowly from our own point of view according to how we see and understand a situation.

Imagine the scene when the younger son goes to tell his father that he wants to leave home. Not only that, he wants his share of the inheritance that would come to him when his father dies. He wants it now! The conversation would probably have been like this.

"Look son, why do you have to leave home? You have everything you need here; please do not make a mess of your life."
But the son insisted, **"No, I must have my share of the property. I want to go away. I want to make my own life."**

The father must then have surely said, **"Son, if you MUST go away, I shall not force you to stay. But, remember, if ever you want to come back and return home, be sure that you will be more than welcome: there will always be your father's heart and wide open arms waiting to welcome you back to YOUR home."**

The Parable continues:

"Not many days later, the younger son gathered all he had and left on his journey into a far country. There, he squandered his property in loose living. And when he had spent everything, a great famine arose in that country, and he began to be in want. So he hired himself to one of the local inhabitants of that country, who sent him into his fields to feed pigs. And he would gladly have fed on the pods that the pigs ate; and no one gave him anything" (Lk. 15:13-16).

Now the son is starving, the so-called friends have fled; he is completely down and out. But when he does come to his senses the first thought that comes into his mind is that of his father, his father's home. **"I will get up and go to my father,"** he says.

KEY WORDS: loose living

No doubt, the father is watching and praying every day for his son's return. He longs, yearns and hopes that his son will come back to him.

The Bible tells us:
"While he was still yet at a distance, his father saw him and had compassion, and ran and embraced him and kissed him."

When his father sees him coming – he does not stop to say, **"Here's my wretched son coming back, I'll teach him."** No, it is not like that at all.

The boy has carefully rehearsed his confession and even before he gets through it, the father interrupts him, as if to say: **"I know, my son, that you are sorry. You do not need to say it; you have come back home, back to your father, this itself is enough!"** All that the father can think of is to heap on his beloved, repentant son symbols and signs of his unconditional welcome, acceptance and love. He did this by saying:

"Bring quickly the best robe and put it on him and put a ring on his finger, and shoes on his feet; and bring the fatted calf and kill it, let us eat and make merry" (Lk. 15:22-23).

If we pause to think deeply, we will see that the whole parable is really about the FATHER, the prodigal love or extravagant love of the father.

When the elder son comes home from his work in the fields he hears music and dancing. He wonders – celebrations, but why? When he hears that his brother is back, the one who squandered all his part of the property in loose living and that his father is now celebrating in a very big way his return, he is angry. He is so deeply hurt he even refuses to enter his home.

Again, it is the father, in his great love, who comes out to plead with his elder son, who asks for, and even demands, justice: "I have served you faithfully all these years and you did not even give me a kid-goat to celebrate with my friends. But for this waster son of yours, who has swallowed up your property – he and his women – you kill the fatted calf!"

It is now that we get the unmistakable message of the parable given to us by the father: **"Son, you are always with me, and all that is mine is yours. It is only fitting to make merry and be glad for this brother of yours was dead, and is alive; he was lost and is found"** (Lk. 15:31-32).

While the elder son was looking for justice, the father's heart was overflowing with **LOVE**.

What is the message for each one of us?

- The elder son does not approve of the younger son and all that he did. But he goes further and does not **ACCEPT HIM**.
- The father does not approve of the younger son's behaviour. There is not a single word to say that he approves of what his son did. **BUT** he unconditionally accepts him as he really is. In his heart, the father still loves his son.
- What the father offers his repentant son is **UNCONDITIONAL ACCEPTANCE**: this is what God always offers each one of us. This is what St. John means when he says **GOD IS LOVE**.

Activities

1. **Discuss: What is the difference between approval and acceptance? Give an example of each to explain the meaning.**

2. **The word 'prodigal' means 'extravagant'. In the parable:**
   a) How was the younger son being 'prodigal'?
   b) How was the father being 'prodigal'?
   c) How was the elder son not being 'prodigal'?
   d) In what ways are we like the elder son?

3. **Work in groups: What is the most important message in the Parable of the Lost Son for YOU? How is it likely to help you? Give an example.**

Deepen our understanding of the Sacrament of Reconciliation.
Reflect on how it can help us to grow in our relationships.

The Sacrament of Reconciliation

Steps to Growth

God is always coming into our lives to help us but frequently we are not aware of **Him coming**.

Study this illustration of Jesus knocking at the door. Have you noticed that there is no handle on it? It is because the artist wants us to understand that Jesus knocks – but waits for us to open to him.

If we are always thinking of ourselves, our needs, what we want, we will not even be aware of God knocking at the door of our heart. We won't even feel our need for God. God will never impose Himself on us. He respects our freedom. I punish myself when I choose to close my heart to God.

Study this picture of Jesus knocking on the door.
Write either a poem or meditation on what you think is happening and will happen.
You or someone else can be inside the house.

Activities

Reconciliation

Reconciliation is a gift from God. God is waiting to help us when we open our heart to Him. He will give us the strength and the courage to say 'sorry' to anyone we have hurt and to forgive those who hurt us.

Steps to Recovery

- Consciously acknowledge what we have done wrong.
- Accept ourselves as a person who had done wrong.
- Open up and surrender ourselves to God so that He can heal us and give us His grace and strength.

What is sin?

Sin is a failure to love God and others. It is deliberately doing what we know to be wrong. There are two types of sin, **MORTAL** and **VENIAL**.

Mortal sin is a very serious sin. It has to be something that is very wrong. The person knows it is very wrong and yet freely chooses to do it.

Venial sin is less serious but we have to make a real effort to avoid committing it.

Confessing mortal sin

When we have committed a mortal sin we need to receive the Sacrament of Reconciliation or, as we often say, go to Confession as soon as possible because we are no longer in the state of grace. We no longer have sanctifying grace which gives us the possibility of eternal life with God.

Confessing without serious sin

The Sacrament of Reconciliation is also available to us when we have not sinned seriously. It helps us to renew and transform our inner lives. It is God's gift of love to heal, renew and strengthen us for everyday living. It is by frequently receiving this sacrament that we will have the courage and strength to hand over our lives to Jesus and become his true disciple. Through this sacrament we receive the grace which brings God fully alive in us – this is called sanctifying grace.

Ways to Confess

Before Confession

1. I think about the times I have turned in on myself and hurt others.

2. I ask for grace to be truly sorry for my sins.

3. I tell God that I want to change and turn back to Him.

At Confession

1. I ask the priest to bless me and say how long it is since my last Confession.

2. I tell him what I have done wrong on purpose.

3. The priest will give me a penance.

4. I tell God that I am really sorry by making an Act of Contrition, that is, saying I am sorry to God and promising, with God's help, to avoid that sin in the future.

5. God forgives me through the words of the priest.

6. I say 'Thank you' to the priest.

After Confession

I say my penance (or think about what the priest has asked me to do).

I thank God for his forgiveness and love.

Activities

1. You, Brian and Gavin have been great friends but Brian and Gavin have said very hurtful things to each other. Gavin believes his friendship with Brian has definitely ended. How could Brian have said such things?

    Obviously, Gavin is deeply wounded. Brian believes that Gavin provoked him to say what he did – so he deserved it!
    a) Look back at the 'Steps to Recovery'.
    b) Plan a way to help both Gavin and Brian.

2. "I have not committed any serious sin so why go to Confession?" asked Jayne. Write an email to Jayne to help her to understand the importance of going to Confession regularly.

Jesus, the Physician

There are many stories in the New Testament which show the love and compassion Jesus has for those who are sick. He even identifies himself with them: **"I was sick and you visited me"** (Mt. 25:36). Jesus explains that what we do to help those who are sick, we do to him and we will be rewarded in heaven for it.

Sometimes, the gospel writers tell us that when Jesus went to a certain village, the people brought all their sick ones from all around that area. The gospel writers simply say that 'many who touched him were cured'.

Did Jesus ask for anything from the people before he cured them?

Jesus often looked for faith and trust before he performed a miracle. For example, a friend of Jesus, called Lazarus, died. By the time Jesus arrived, he had been dead four days. His sisters, Martha and Mary, were weeping. When Jesus told people to roll away the stone from Lazarus' grave, Martha said that the body would have started to decay. Jesus reminded her: "Have I not told you that if you believe you will see the glory of God?" (Jn. 11:40).

Does Jesus heal everyone who believes?

No, but Jesus helps everyone who believes and trusts in him. The problem of suffering is a very great mystery. A mystery is a truth which we cannot understand; it is something which is hidden from our eyes. We sometimes wonder why God allows little children to suffer and die. 'There are no quick answers. The mystery of God is too great, and our minds too small, too limited to understand His ways" (Cardinal Basil Hume).

Even though a person may not be cured physically, when they believe and trust in the power of Jesus they receive an inner peace, a tranquility which helps them to cope. When they receive the Sacrament of the Sick they may not be cured but they receive an inner strength, a peace which strengthens their belief in God and they know that one day they will see Him face to face and be with Him in heaven.

Research the following miracles of Jesus curing the sick and raising the dead.

Your teacher will give you a diagram. Use it to explain what prompted Jesus to help the people and what it tells us about him.

John 9:1-7	Luke 8:49-56
Mark 2:1-12	Luke 7:1-10
Luke 7:11-16	Luke 5:12-14

**Know about the Sacrament of the Sick.
Reflect on how it can help us.**

A True Story

The hospital ward was busy. It was operating day again. Peggy had had her operation three days earlier and was well on the way to recovery so she was able to take stock of all the hustle and bustle. The nurses were busy with their routine duties; surgeons were visiting their patients, doing a final check. Patients were looking quite nervous.

Suddenly, Peggy noticed the calm figure of a priest walking up the ward towards her bed. He wanted to know if she would like to receive Holy Communion the following morning. She was delighted and wondered if she was the only Catholic on the ward.

A few hours later, the staff-nurse came to ask her if a lady from Ward B could join her for the Holy Communion service. She explained that the lady was from Dublin and had been taken very ill while on holidays.

The next morning, Mary came to join Peggy. As soon as the priest had left, Mary shared what she felt with Peggy: "Going to Mass is one thing," she said, "but to think the great God of Heaven would seek us out in this place and come to us Himself - that beats everything."

A few hours later, the surgeon told Mary that she had inoperable cancer and that nothing could be done for her. In the days that followed the two women shared a lot. Peggy was deeply touched by Mary's faith in God.

On the third day, Mary had a bad turn and the priest came to anoint her. She was put in a corner bed with the screens drawn but that did not exclude the noise of the ward. Peggy was allowed to visit her and still remembers the experience: "I found her holding her crucifix, her lips moving as she struggled through the rosary. She could still smile a little and told me: 'I've learnt something. she said. The good Lord was almost alone when He was dying. I never thought of that before. So here, away from my own home, I'm sharing that with Him, bless Him.'" As Peggy sat beside her bed she knew that Mary had received a great grace through the Sacrament of the Sick. She was calm; she knew she would not get better but she believed she was going to be with the good Lord.

All who had come to see Mary were amazed to find her so peaceful. Her family and friends, even though they were upset, were able to pray with her and reflect on what they must do in order to have faith and trust in God like her. Mary died a few weeks later.

Activities

1   a) **What did Mary receive through the Sacrament of the Sick?**
    b) **In what way do you think she may have helped her friends and relations?**

The Sacrament of the Sick

When a person is receiving the sacrament the priest blesses those present with holy water. There is a short penitential rite and a reading from scripture. Everyone prays in silence as the priest lays hands on the head of the sick person.

The priest calls on the power of the Holy Spirit to heal him or her.

The priest anoints the sick person's forehead and the palms of the hands with blessed oil.

Priest: Through this holy anointing may the Lord, in His love and mercy, help you with the grace of the Holy Spirit.
All: Amen.
Priest: May the Lord who frees you from sin save you and raise you up.
All: Amen.

The priest says a special prayer for the sick person and then everyone joins in to say the Lord's Prayer. The priest gives Holy Communion. The ceremony ends with a final prayer and blessing.

Where is the sacrament celebrated?

The sacrament may be celebrated in private or in public.
In private: at home, in hospital, in a hospice or in a nursing home with family and friends.
In public: in the local church, at Mass for sick people of the parish or during a pilgrimage, for example, in Lourdes.

Who should receive the sacrament?

An adult or a child may receive the Sacrament of the Sick:
- when he or she is seriously ill;
- when he or she is going to have a major operation;
- when a person is old and very weak.

A person may be anointed as many times as necessary in his/her life.

How does the sacrament help people?

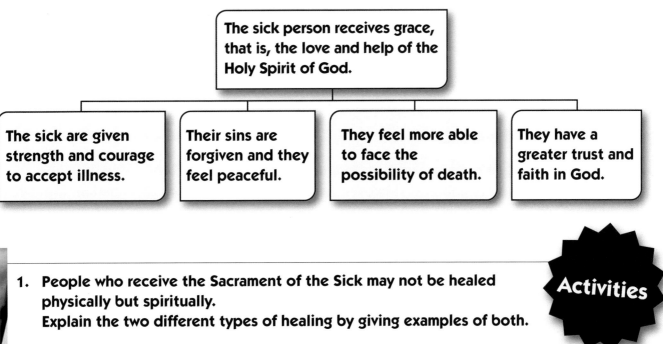

The sick person receives grace, that is, the love and help of the Holy Spirit of God.

The sick are given strength and courage to accept illness.

Their sins are forgiven and they feel peaceful.

They feel more able to face the possibility of death.

They have a greater trust and faith in God.

Activities

1. People who receive the Sacrament of the Sick may not be healed physically but spiritually.
   Explain the two different types of healing by giving examples of both.

2. Imagine you have a friend who is a Catholic and about to undergo major surgery. Write a letter to explain what the Sacrament of the Sick is and how it will help should he/she wish to receive it. Think about:
   - what happens in the Sacrament of the Sick;
   - where the person can receive it;
   - how the Sacrament helps;
   - advice on how to prepare for it.

3. Some people feel their prayers are not answered. Using what you have learnt in this section write a response to them.

6. Christianity & Other Faiths

Know that Christianity continues to spread throughout the world. Reflect on the experience and example of St. Paul.

Overwhelmed by Events

Try to think of the most joyful experience you have ever had in your life. How did it affect you? Who did you share it with? Do you still want to share it now?

The most baffling and overwhelming experience for the Apostles was when the Holy Spirit burst upon them at Pentecost. They simply became 'drunk' with the deepest possible joy one could imagine. Because they had received the tremendous conviction that **Jesus** was truly **GOD**.

Their conviction was so blinding that they never again could turn from Him. Not only that, but at that moment, there was given to them a courage, freedom and bravery that was going to influence the rest of their lives. They would tell everyone about the risen Jesus with courage, conviction and fearlessness no matter what obstacles they met.

God's power works best

St. Paul was the greatest missionary of his time. He was very intelligent, articulate and capable of winning every argument. However, he discovered that when he relied on himself, on his own powers, to win over people, they just stifled yawns and told him that they would listen to him another time. He had an important lesson to learn: he had to rely on God and put total trust in Him.

Paul reflects on his experience

Paul realised that wherever he had gone to teach about Jesus there had been suffering and yet the number of believers grew. He understood that when his suffering was greatest, he opened his heart to God, pleading for help. Gradually he understood that God worked best; God's power was greatest when he totally relied on Him.

What does Paul teach us?

It is when we trust in God and put ourselves totally in His hands that that everything will eventually work out best for us.

Paul's strong advice

Paul warns us that trusting in God does not mean we can just acknowledge we are weak, powerless or not intelligent and rely on God to do the work for us. That is the last thing he wants us to do, because it would make us lazy. That is not the will of God for us.

What does Paul want?

What Paul wants us to understand is that, when we feel weak and inadequate, we should plead with God to help us to succeed. We can be sure that God will give us everything that He wants to give us when we hold on to Him and open up our heart to receive Him. This is what many of the great missionaries did and this is why Christianity has spread throughout the world today.

St. Augustine said: "Pray as if everything depended on God. Act as if everything depended on you".

Activities

1. a)   What do you think was the greatest lesson St. Paul had to learn?
   b)   What does he want us to learn from his experience?
   c)   Explain in your own words the advice St. Augustine gives us. Give an example.

2.   It is said that St. Paul was the greatest missionary of his time. Do you agree? Write an essay. Some points to guide you:
   • What type of character was he? Who or what formed his character?
   • What lessons did he have to learn? Who taught him?
   • What do you think about the result of his missionary work?
   • Where did he travel?
   • What difficulties did he encounter?
   • What successes did he have?

Spread of Christianity

"Go out into the whole world and proclaim the Good News" (Mt. 28:19).

This was the command that Jesus gave to the Apostles. This command has been passed on to all Christians including us.

Since that time, religious men, women and lay people have gone to all corners of the world to bring the Good News. They have done this in a variety of ways: as priests, brothers, nuns, nurses, doctors, teachers and people with a variety of other skills.

The Jesuits, Franciscans, Columbans, Missionaries of Africa and many other religious orders, are all over the world. They have universities, schools, centres of spirituality, retreats centres and are involved in working with lay people to reach out to help young and old who are in need.

Christianity is still growing. We asked some people why they think this is the case. Here are some of their replies:

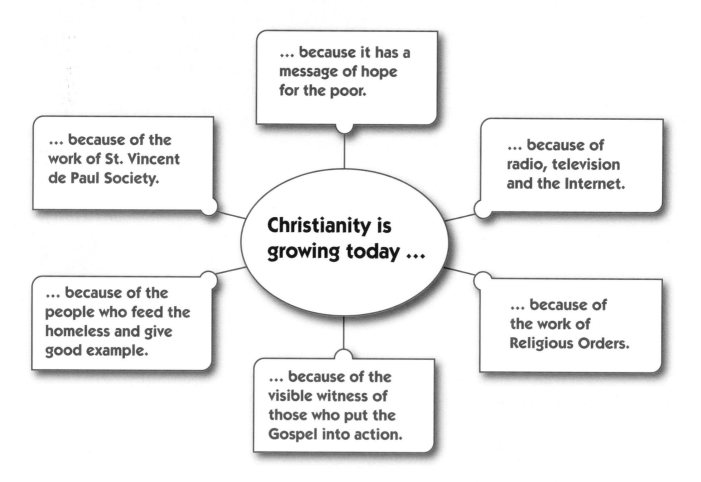

... because it has a message of hope for the poor.

... because of the work of St. Vincent de Paul Society.

... because of radio, television and the Internet.

Christianity is growing today ...

... because of the people who feed the homeless and give good example.

... because of the work of Religious Orders.

... because of the visible witness of those who put the Gospel into action.

BUZZ SESSION: Who do you think contributes to the growth of Christianity today? Try to give examples of how their contributions have enabled Christianity to grow.

Great Missionaries

We are now going to look at the lives of some of these great missionaries to see how God worked through them.

St. Francis Xavier

St. Francis Xavier was a Spanish Jesuit. In 1541, he set out on a mission to India and, after thirteen months of sailing, he arrived in Goa. From there he went to south east India spreading the Gospel among the very poor people. Everywhere he went he encountered difficulties but a fire burned within him to teach as many people as possible about Jesus. He baptised tens of thousands of people.

In 1549, he was the first missionary to go to Japan. Unfortunately, he did not know the language and his Japanese interpreter was not able to find words to explain the truths of Christianity so there were not many conversions. In 1552, he set out for China. This was a country completely closed to foreigners. His plans did not work out: on 3 December he died on an island all alone, except for a Chinese man who put a lighted candle into his hands.

In spite of all the difficulties and setbacks, thousands of conversions are attributed to Francis Xavier. His strength was in prayer. He handed over his life to God. He knew that, in opening his heart to God and completely trusting in Him, God's power could work in situations that humanly speaking were impossible. He took particular care of the sick, the poor and children. He has taught us that we must never give up when there are difficulties and failures: these are the springboard for placing all our faith and trust in God.

Over the last four centuries, an extraordinary number of young Jesuits have volunteered to go to India to continue the work of St. Francis Xavier. They keep in mind the belief that Francis had: one should never be discouraged by failures, even the worst difficulties, but place all one's hope and faith in God and seek every human means to help people to know and love Jesus.

Today, in China there are almost thirty million Christians. They cannot openly practise their faith and at times bishops have been put under house arrest, in police custody or in hiding – but their faith and trust in God are powerful.

The Martyrs of Uganda

King Mwanga of Buganda became very jealous and angry when he realised that the Christian missionaries taught the people to put loyalty to Jesus before loyalty to the king. He forbade anyone to go near a Christian mission on pain of death. The converts to Christianity refused to obey him.

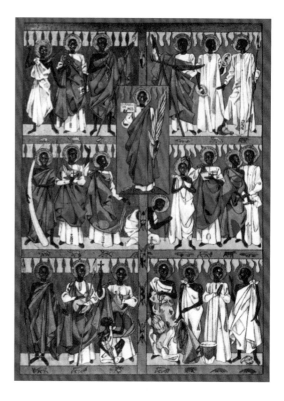

He was determined to wipe out Christianity. He ordered thirty-two young men, who were pages in his court, to renounce Christianity. They refused and the King condemned them to death by burning.

On 3 June 1866, these martyrs walked to their death singing hymns and praying for their enemies. Their courage and faith in God inspired very many people who looked on at what was happening. They were so touched by the witness of these young men that they too became Christians.

Within a few years, the original handful of converts had multiplied many times and spread far and wide throughout Uganda. Today, Uganda is rated as having the highest percentage of Christians of any nation in Africa.

Activities

1. a) Write down two of the challenges St. Francis Xavier had to face.
   b) Briefly describe the successes and disappointments that came with the challenges.
   c) What do you think many people inherited from him?

2. In spite of the attempts made to wipe out Christianity from Uganda, it is flourishing. What explanations could you give for this?

3. 'Complete freedom to be a Christian does not help.' Discuss
   a) Say what you think and why;
   b) give a different point of view and say why some people may hold it;
   c) say why you disagree with it;
   d) quote some source of evidence.

KEY WORDS: martyr, pages

Venerable Edel Quinn: a Modern Witness

Edel Quinn is one of the outstanding missionaries of the 20th century and, hopefully, will soon be canonized. She was born in County Cork in the south of Ireland, on 14 September 1907. In 1932, she entered the Order of the Poor Clares and was soon diagnosed with an incurable disease so she left the monastery.

She spent the next eighteen months trying to get better. When she realised her health was not improving she decided to do something useful with her life before she died. She was a member of the Legion of Mary and was asked to go to East Africa as a missionary. She said goodbye to her family and friends knowing she would not be returning.

For the next eight years, Edel worked in Nairobi, in Kenya, and from there, despite her very poor health, she travelled thousands of miles. The journeys were along rough dirt tracks to Uganda, Tanzania, Malawi, Zimbabwe, South Africa and even to Mauritius in the Indian Ocean.

With another companion, Edel went out into villages and hillsides, teaching children and adults all about Jesus and preparing them to become Catholics. She also spent much time visiting the sick and the dying. She set up new groups of the Legion of Mary and one of these was for people with leprosy.

Frequently, she was laid low by poor health: malaria, pneumonia and sheer exhaustion. But her will-power, forgetfulness of herself, her commitment and desire to tell everybody about Jesus was the driving force of her life. She knew she was receiving her strength from the Eucharist.

After several very long journeys to various parts of Africa, Edel's life was cut short by a series of heart-attacks and she died on 12 May 1944 with the words of **"Jesus, Jesus, I love you"** on her lips.

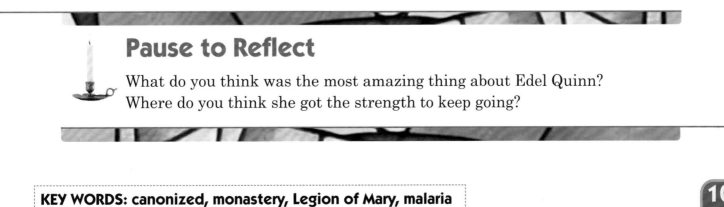

Pause to Reflect

What do you think was the most amazing thing about Edel Quinn?
Where do you think she got the strength to keep going?

Gladys Aylward: Missionary to China

Gladys Aylward was born in London about 1904. She worked for several years as a maid in the home of a well-to-do family. One day, she attended a meeting where the preacher called on people to dedicate their lives to the service of God. Gladys responded to the call and became convinced that God meant her to preach the Gospel to the people of China. The Chinese people at that time distrusted foreigners and did not want to hear about Christianity.

After some time, Gladys went to help an elderly missionary in the small town of Yangchen. The two women decided to set up an inn and provide hospitality to travellers and to tell them stories in the evening about a man named Jesus. This proved a success and some Chinese became Christians.

Gladys became fluent in the local language and lived and dressed like the people around her. Gradually they learned to trust her and accept her help. She stopped a riot in the prison and improved conditions for the men imprisoned there. She started an orphanage for abandoned and unwanted children. The people began to call her 'Ai-weh-deh' which means 'Virtuous One.' The Mandarin of Yangchen eventually announced that he was impressed by her way of life and wished to become a Christian.

In 1938, Japan and China were at war. Japanese planes bombed Yangchen. The Mandarin advised survivors to flee into the mountains. Gladys was reluctant to go but when she heard that the Japanese had put a price on her head she had to leave. She decided to seek safety for her orphans and herself at Sian.

For twelve days, Gladys walked across the mountains with a hundred children from her orphanage. Finally they reached the Yellow River, but there was no boat to cross it. The children and Gladys knelt and prayed. Then they sang. A Chinese officer heard them and managed to arrange for a boat to ferry them across the river. No sooner had they reached the government orphanage which welcomed all the children when Gladys collapsed with typhus fever.

Her work was not over! As soon as the war ended Gladys worked at a settlement for lepers near the border of China and Tibet. When her health failed, she returned to England and died in January 1970.

1. Make a diagram to summarise the life of Gladys Alyward using bullet points under the following headings:
    Acts of Faith Gladys made;
    Challenges she encountered;
    Blessings she received.

2. Reflect on the four stories in this section.
    a) Choose the one you think was the greatest witness to the teaching of Jesus.
    b) Give reasons and examples for your choice. It may help to think of the following:
    *   a person's relationship with Jesus;
    *   public witness;
    *   perseverance when confronted with difficulties;
    *   what you think enabled the person to keep going;
    *   what you will want to remember about that person.

3. We have seen how God works through people in different ways. Think about your own life and how you would like God to work through you. Be imaginative.
    *   Draw a path and along it write what you would like to do to help others.
    *   Focus on every ten years of your life, for example age 12, 22, 32.
    *   Mention what you need to do in order to experience God's greatest power.

Know what the Catholic Church teaches about other Faiths.
Think of ways in which we can work with young people of other Faiths.

What We Believe

We live in a multi-faith and multi-cultural society, so there is a very great need for us to know about other faiths and to be able to share with them.

However, we have to understand our own faith before we can truly share with others. If we are uncertain about what we believe it will lead to confusion. It is only when we have a clear understanding of **WHAT WE BELIEVE** and **WHY WE BELIEVE IT** that we can have really interesting discussions with young people of other faiths because we have something to share with them.
This is what Archbishop Vincent Nichols said:

"When we approach other faiths we do so in the spirit of 'walking on holy ground'. As Catholics we are committed to respecting other faiths as arenas in which God is at work."

Let us try to draw together all the essential truths that we have been studying this year and make links with other Faiths.

Points of Catholic Faith

- There is only one God, creator of all people and things.
- In God alone do all people find unending happiness.
- God's plan is to save all people without exception.
- Jesus is the one mediator between God and people.
- Jesus is the one and only Saviour of all people.
- All who are saved – whether Christians, Jews, Muslims or others – are saved through the grace of God even when they do not know it.

What does the Catholic Church teach about Other Faiths?

- The gift of God's grace is absolutely free and available to everyone.
- God has spoken and continues to speak in a variety of ways.
- There is a variety of ways in which human beings respond to God's grace.
- God's Holy Spirit has been at work in all religious traditions.
- There are elements of truth and goodness in other religions
- All the goodness in the minds and hearts of people of other faiths is deeply respected by the Catholic Church.

We All Belong to God

As humans, we differ in many ways: skin colour, language, gender, intellectual and physical abilities and also our religious beliefs. Yet we are all created by God.

The Church teaches that there is only one community and it consists of all people. We all belong to God and we have one final destiny – GOD – His goodness and plan for salvation extend to all people.

"People turn to various religions to solve mysteries of the human condition, which today, as in earlier times, burden people's hearts: the nature of man; the meaning and purpose of life; good and evil; the origin and purpose of suffering; the way to true happiness; death, judgement ...."

(Pope John Paul II "Crossing the Threshold of Hope, p78).

The Catholic Church *"rejects nothing that is true and holy in these religions"*. The Church has a high regard for their conduct and way of life. The Church believes and teaches that these religions *"often reflect a ray of that truth which enlightens all people"* (Nostra Aetate para. 2).

Does it matter which Faith we believe in?

- **The Catholic Church firmly believes that Jesus is the Way, the Truth and the Life.**
- **We have received the gift of Divine Revelation which has made known to us that Jesus is God and through HIM we go to God.**
- **Jesus came into the world for all people; he has HIS own way of reaching others.**
- **The Church is the Body of Jesus Christ.**
- **The Church is the People of God.**
- **Jesus has promised to be with the Church until the end of time.**

Activities

1. a) Prepare for MASTERMIND. You may work in pairs.
   You have a choice of three topics.
   (i) Points of Catholic Faith;
   (ii) What the Catholic Church teaches about other Faiths;
   (iii) Does it matter what we believe?
   Choose one topic as your specialist subject. For the other two topics, write down questions based on the information above.

   b) MASTERMIND
   Pupils take turns of being in the Spotlight (answering questions) and others asking the questions.

2. Here are some questions you are likely to be asked by people of other faiths.
   Work in small groups to prepare a leaflet or booklet with the answers.
   a) What is the Church?
   b) How does someone become a member of the Church?
   c) What are the most important beliefs that Catholics hold? (Reference: The Creed)
   d) What are the major events that the Catholic Church celebrates?

The Spirit of God is at work

The Spirit of God shows us that the diversity of gifts among Christians and people of other faiths is a blessing for all of us. We are now witnessing, in different parts of our country and in many parts of the world, how people of all faiths are working together to help those less fortunate than ourselves and for the care of the environment. This was expressed in a shared act of reflection and commitment by the faith communities of the United Kingdom at the official opening of the Millennium celebrations:

In a world scarred by the evils of war, racism, injustice and poverty, the leaders of many faiths made this joint Act of Commitment.

We commit ourselves,
as people of many faiths,
to work together
for the common good,
uniting to build a better society,
grounded in values and ideals we share:
community,
personal integrity,
a sense of right and wrong,
learning, wisdom and love of truth,
care and compassion,
justice and peace,
respect for one another,
for the earth and its creatures.

We commit ourselves,
in a spirit of friendship and co-operation,
to work together
alongside all who share our values and
ideals,
to help bring about a better world
now and for generations to come.

Faith In Action

1. **Some pupils who are Muslims were asked to give examples of how their beliefs affect their behaviour. This is what they said:**

> I pray three times a day. This helps me to remember that I depend on Allah's help and need to thank him.

> During the month of Ramadan, my beliefs affect my behaviour because I fast during the day to concentrate my mind on good things that I should be grateful to Allah for.

If asked by a Muslim how your beliefs affect your behaviour what would you say?

2. **Work in pairs or small groups. Write your own Act of Commitment. Use your ICT skills to type it out so that it can be used for display in the classroom or corridor.**

> **Be aware of some of the major world religions.**
> **Reflect on some values we share with them.**

Some Major World Religions

In the United Kingdom, there is a growing number of religions. People from all over the world come to live here and bring with them their faiths and cultures. As Christians, while it is very important that we have a very good understanding of our own faith and beliefs, it is also essential that we have some knowledge and understanding of other major world religions.

In 2001, a census was taken in **Britain** to find out the number of people belonging to world religions. Here are the findings:

Buddhists:	152,000
Jews:	267,000
Sikhs:	336,000
Hindus:	559,000
Muslims:	1,591,000
Christians:	42,079,000
Other:	179,000

'Other' came from a wide variety of different religions.

While there are many world religions, in this book we are only able to mention some of them.

HINDUISM is the oldest of the world religions and dates to about 2500 B.C. (before the birth of Jesus Christ). It includes a vast variety of beliefs and many sects to which the majority of the people of India belong. According to Hindu belief, individuals are born into one of five castes (social classes) based on their good or bad deeds (karma) in a past life. Through meditation and good living the person may advance to another caste in his or her next life. Mohandas Gandhi is the most famous modern Hindu leader. He was known as Mahatma (the Great Soul).

JUDAISM began with God's call to Abraham and developed about 2000 BC. It teaches belief in one God. This God is loving, merciful and forgiving and entered into a special covenant with his 'Chosen People'. This covenant required the Jews to follow God's laws, including those given to Moses on Mount Sinai. The Jews believe that the Messiah is still to come.

SIKHISM started around the 15th Century by Guru Nanak.
Sikhs believe in one God who created the universe and is present in creation and in each human being. God is the only eternal reality who will remain after all life disappears. They meditate on the many names for God, such as, Waheguru (Wonderful Lord), Satnam (the Eternal Reality) and Akal Purakh (the Eternal One).

ISLAM started over 600 years after the birth of Jesus Christ, that is, 600 AD. It began in Saudi Arabia through the Prophet Mohammed. Muslims worship one God, Allah, who is revealed to them in the Koran, their sacred text. Mohammed, who was born in Mecca, is seen as Allah's prophet and messenger. Their faith provides guidelines and rules for all aspects of life. Their God is awesome, just, loving and merciful. They pray five times a day, give alms and fast during the ninth month of the Muslim year.

KEY WORDS: sect, Messiah

BUDDHISM was started in India during the 6th century AD by Siddhartha Gautama, known as Buddha or Enlightened One. Most Buddhists do not believe in God. Their religion teaches the practice of meditation and rules for good behaviour. It claims that people are reincarnated, that is, that they come back to earth in another form when they die. It holds that people are happy or sad depending on their actions (karma) in a previous life.

Values We Share

We share many values with people of other faiths. Here are some examples of how we should treat each other:

Hinduism:
"This is the sum of duty: do not do to others what would cause pain if done to you" (Mahabharata 5:15-17).

Judaism:
"...thou shalt love thy neighbour as thyself" (Leviticus 19:18).
"Do to no one what you would not want done to you" (Tobit 4:15).

Islam:
"None of you [truly] believes until he wishes for his brother what he wishes for himself" (Number 13 of Imam 'Al-Nawawi's Forty Hadiths').

Christianity:
"So always treat others as you would like them to treat you; that is the meaning of the Law and the Prophets" (Matthew 7:12).
"Love your enemies, do good to those who hate you, bless those who curse you, pray for those who treat you badly" (Luke 6:27).

Sikhism:
"Compassion, mercy and religion are the support of the entire world" (Japji Sahib).
"Don't create enmity with anyone as God is within everyone" (Guru Arjan Devji 259).
"No one is my enemy, none a stranger and everyone is my friend" (Guru Arjan Dev: AG 1299).

Buddhism:
"Just as a mother would protect her only child with her life, even so let one cultivate a boundless love towards all beings" (Khuddaka Patha, from the Metta Sutta).

1. a) Read the stories that your teacher will give you:
      • Testing Virtue – Buddhism;
      • Six Blind Men and the Elephant - Hinduism;
      • What Should I Do? – Islam;
      • The Good and the Bad - Sikhism.
    b) Choose one story. Write out the most important message that the story conveys.
    c) What do you think we can learn from it?
    d) Write your own story to illustrate your values.

2. Research: Your teacher will give you a letter between (a) – (g). Research the task which matches your letter. Share your findings with the rest of the class.

    a) What are the Four Noble Truths of Buddhism?

    b) What are two of the most important beliefs of Hinduism?

    c) What are two of the most important beliefs of Sikhism?

    d) Explain what the symbol 'Menorah' means for Jews.

    e) Who are the three major historical figures that Jews and Christians share?

    f) Which books of the Bible are included in the Torah?

    g) What do Muslims do during the month of Ramadan? Why?

3. Five groups: Each group has a different religion and researches aspects of it.
    a) Look at the list of aspects and write down what you know about your chosen religion.
    b) Write down what you want to know.
    c) Use www.REonline.org (Key Stage 2) or other websites to help you learn more about it.
    d) When finished, make a presentation to the other groups of the religion you have studied.
    e) Make a display for the classroom.

RELIGIONS
Buddhism
Hinduism
Islam
Judaism
Sikhism

ASPECTS
Beliefs
People
Places
Sacred Writings
Special Days
Symbols
Worship
History of Religions

Bonds of Friendship

How often do we turn on the television and see story after story about conflict and problems around the world? A bomb has gone off and often a religious fanatic is the cause. This can give Christians, Muslims, Hindus or any religious group a bad name even though they have nothing to do with the terrorist attack.

We are going to reflect on the importance of getting to know people of other faiths and finding ways of working with them but let's start by reading about some of the great bonds of friendship that have existed.

Memories of two boys

The two boys – one Jewish, the other Christian, were friends, neighbours, classmates in Wadowice, Poland. Together they played soccer, visited one another's families, did their homework together. It was wonderful until World War II (1939 - 1945) separated them.

The Jewish boy went to serve in the Polish army following the German invasion of his country. He survived, but lived to see most of his family die in Nazi death camps. Meanwhile, his Christian friend went to study to be a priest. At that time, the seminaries in Poland had to officially close because the German army occupied the country and cracked down on the Church. However, they operated secretly: this was known as the 'underground' seminary.

But the bonds of friendship and respect that Jerzy Kluger and Karol Wojtyla had formed as boys in wartime Poland were too strong to be broken by separation, distance and differences. After almost thirty years, the two men were reunited in Rome. It was there Mr. Kluger settled after the war and where, by chance, he heard a news report about a young Polish archbishop who had spoken eloquent words during the Second Vatican Council.

Mr. Kluger lost no time. He telephoned the Vatican and the two men – one a business man, the other an archbishop who would go on to be the pope – resumed their friendship.

After that, Mr. Kluger worked with Pope John Paul II to strengthen relations between Jews and Christians. Pope John Paul II said: **"As Christians and Jews, following the example of the faith of Abraham, we are called to be a blessing for the world. This is the common task awaiting us. It is therefore necessary for us, Christians and Jews, to be first a blessing to one another."**

1. What to you think were the memories that Mr. Kluger and Pope John Paul shared? Do some research on the Internet to support your views.

2. Research what Pope John Paul II did to support the Jews, for example, his pilgrimage to Israel, March 2000.

Cardinal Basil Hume

Cardinal Hume, who died on 17th June, 1999, was the leader of the Catholic Church in England and Wales for more than twenty years. He was regarded by many as Britain's most popular religious leader. He reached out to people of all faiths and had many great friends among them.

The British Muslim community expressed its deep grief and sense of loss on hearing that the Cardinal had died. "As members of the Abrahamic faith community, British Muslims sincerely grieve the passing away of the British Catholic leader, Cardinal Basil Hume and we wish to condole and share with you, your as well as our sense of loss, over the demise of this noble and 'respected personality.' "

The Chief Rabbi Jonathan Sacks of the United Hebrew Congregations of the Commonwealth said,

When I think of Cardinal Hume, I recall the words of Judaism's early wise men. 'They asked: 'Who is a hero?' They answered: 'One who turns strangers into friends'. As a monk and the leader of Britain's Catholic community, Cardinal Hume attracted people from a wide variety of backgrounds and drew them to a deeper love of God.

The Chief Rabbi formed a bond of friendship with Cardinal Hume. Even though many of their religious beliefs were different, they shared similar views about the problems people had to face in life.

They enjoyed being together and when Cardinal Hume died in 1999, the Chief Rabbi felt he had lost a great friend. As a Rabbi, he could not take part in the funeral at Westminster Cathedral. Instead, he went to the Archbishop's house next door and spent the time in prayer. By doing this, he honoured the memory of his friend without breaking the rule of his own faith.

Pause to Reflect

- What were some of the religious beliefs that Cardinal Basil Hume and Rabbi Jonathan Sacks did not hold in common?
- What do you think helped to strengthen their bond of friendship?
- What can we learn from them?

Catholic father – Muslim mother:
a true story by Fr. Renato Oliveros S.J.

Many years ago, my Muslim mother did a very brave thing when she married my father, who was a Catholic. Her family disowned her but one day she went home to visit her parents taking her two sons with her. Grandpa forgave and accepted my father into the family. It was the happiest period in my mother's life.

God was so real to my mother. She practised zakat (charity) faithfully as she always had something to share with the poor. She taught me that we have to care for God's poor the best way we can. This made a lasting impression on me. It was through my mother's generosity and faith in Allah, that God first became so real; not just a transcendent God divorced from the suffering of people – but a God who cares.

At the University of the Philippines campus, I was upset by evangelical groups who preached that, unless one accepts Jesus as a personal saviour, one is not saved. I was worried about my Muslim mother. In a panic, I went for advice to a Jesuit priest who was also a student at the university. I told him that I was determined to convert my mother to Christianity because of my fear that she might not be 'saved'. But instead of approving of what I wanted to do, I got a scolding from this priest. He said: "If God called your mother to be a Muslim let her be a good Muslim. You need to respect her belief."
This helped me to understand that God's salvation is for all. The Church has stated that God draws all people to Himself.

"God's goodness and plans for salvation are extended to all" (Nostra Aetate, para. 1).

KEY WORDS: evangelical groups, salvation, revelation

The day I told my mother that I was joining the Jesuits, she smiled and said: "Although I am a Muslim, I am happy for you. I grant you my blessings and prayers."

In the Philippines where I live, the Muslims know I am a Catholic priest. Also, they have heard that my mother is a Muslim. This has not caused any problems; in fact they even respect me because they know that I also work for God. I am now teaching at Manila University where there are many Muslims. Their commitment to prayers reminds me to organize my own life around prayer. The threat from some religious fanatics in the Philippines is a struggle for those who believe that God is a God of Peace (As-Salaam/Pax Christi), and a God who abhors violence. Peace is not simply a gift, it is an important task.

Activities

1. **Read again the true story of Fr. Renato. Use bullet points to list all the things you have learnt from this story.**
   Why is this story so exceptional?

2. **We have seen examples of bonds of good friendship between people of the different faiths. Here are some suggestions on how to do this from Year 8 pupils.**

If people heed their commandments they should live together in peace and harmony.	Have an inter-faith project where we all work together to help the less advantaged.	Create centres which enable young people of all faiths to become calm and still.

   a) **Can you suggest ways in which we can develop good relationships and work together?**

   b) **If you have friends among people of other faiths write about what you share and what you do together. Is there anything you cannot share?**

   c) **If none of your friends is from another faith, imagine you have a friend who is either a Muslim or a Jew. What would you enjoy doing together? Would there be any obstacles to your friendship because of your faith?**

Mahatma Gandhi

Mahatma Gandhi was born on 2 October 1869 in Porbander, India. He became one of the most respected spiritual and political leaders of his time. He helped free the Indian people from British rule through non-violent resistance and is honoured by his people as the father of the Indian Nation.

A True Story by an Indian Jesuit Priest

As a young university student in Bombay around the year 1945, I had the grace and joy of coming in contact with Mahatma (means 'great soul') Gandhi. I was deeply inspired by him. At that time, he was leading our nation, India, in a wholly non-violent way to freedom and independence.

We heard that Gandhi was in Bombay at the time and would be holding his prayer-meetings for a couple of weeks on the shores of the Arabian Sea.

I had heard and read of Gandhi and was personally enchanted with this holy 'man-of-God' who was leading our country to freedom. As a student then, I finished my practicals (mathematics and science) early and rushed to get a place on the beach where I knew there would be thousands of people waiting to listen to and pray with Gandhi.

Gandhi was small and very frail and would sit on a slightly raised dais (platform) on the beach. We crowded around him squatting on the beach. Quite frequently, he would begin by reading a brief passage from Jesus' Sermon on the Mount, the Beatitudes, in St. Matthew's Gospel. He would comment briefly on the words he had read aloud, saying, for example: "Here is where I am learning my non-violence and holding on to truth from this Jesus". And then, he would fall silent and enter deeply into prayer, just repeating quietly over and over again the name of God, "Hari Ram, Hari Ram". After praying with the name of God he would fall into a deep and profound silence. Then, literally, the entire crowd around him – mostly tens of thousands – would be intensely united in praying with this 'man-of-God'. You could hear a pin drop!

After a long period, when all the people and Gandhi had been in silent prayer, this 'man-of-God' would quietly stand up, bow his head and join his hands with the words "NAMASTE" (greeting), and then silently slip away. I was profoundly impressed to note that, one by one, the crowd moved out (businessmen, workers, students, etc.) to catch a train, a bus, a car, or just keep walking, with heads bowed and in deep silence.

On 30th January 1948, Gandhi was returning from his usual daily morning prayer in the company of a couple of his closest friends and was stopped on his way by a person who approached him, seemingly to thank him, but who then pulled out a gun and shot him directly. Gandhi collapsed dead while breathing the name of God: 'Hari Ram'. God's holy name had become the prayer of his heart, of his entire life.

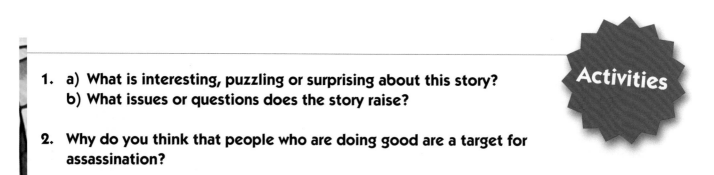

Activities

1. a) **What is interesting, puzzling or surprising about this story?**
    b) **What issues or questions does the story raise?**

2. **Why do you think that people who are doing good are a target for assassination?**

3. **Find out about one or two people who were assassinated for doing good.**

4. **"Young people should learn that violence is not a method for settling disputes."**
    Prepare for a debate or Discuss.

Glossary

Abide – to stay with

Absolve – to forgive completely

Absolution – complete forgiveness of sins

Adultery – to be unfaithful to one's husband or wife

Advent – four week season of prayer, penance and preparation for Christmas

Angels – pure spiritual beings who worship and serve God continually

Anoint – to smear or pour oil on the head as a sign that God has specially chosen that person

Apostle – 'one sent out' to preach the good news

Ark of the Covenant – the chest in which Moses placed the two stone tablets containing the Ten Commandments. The Hebrews treasured it as the most sacred sign of God's presence among them

Ascension – the return of Jesus to his Father in heaven, forty days after his resurrection from death

Authority – the power to settle a question, particularly in religious matters, e.g. the meaning of scripture

Baffling - puzzling, mystifying

Baptism – the rite or sacrament of initiation into the Christian Church

Barren – unable to have children

Bind – to make as law

Bishop – a leader, teacher and guide for God's people (the Church) in a certain area called a diocese

Blasphemy – irreverent or false speech about holy things, e.g. swearing or cursing

Blessed Sacrament – Jesus Christ's body, the consecrated crated host, which is usually reserved (kept safely) in the tabernacle

Bread of Presence – it was an offering, often a food, made to God by the people in their local shrine

Canonize – when the Church makes someone who has died a saint

Cardinal – a cardinal is next in rank to the pope and acts as his adviser and is usually in charge of a large diocese

Carmelite – a member of the order of nuns of Our Lady of Mount Carmel

Catacombs – underground passages along which the dead of ancient Rome were buried; Christians met there for worship in times of persecution

Catechumen – a person who is being instructed in the basic teaching of the Christian faith and is preparing for Baptism

Catechumenate – the period of time in which people prepare for the Sacrament of Baptism

Chosen People – the Israelites (Jews) were chosen by God to play a unique role in world history

Chrism – a perfumed oil used for anointing

Christ – another word for Messiah; both mean 'Anointed One' in English

Commandments – the laws given by God to Moses

Commitment – constant effort and enthusiasm for a cause

Conceive – to become pregnant

Confession – speaking out sins to God; also a name for the Sacrament of Reconciliation

Confessional – small room in which a person confesses their sins to a priest

Convent – a building occupied by a community of religious women

Conscience – our inner voice that tells us right from wrong

Covenant – a solemn promise between two people or groups of people, e.g. God's covenant with Abraham

Crypt – cellar, basement

Curé – Parish Priest

Deities – gods

Descendants – ancestors, genealogy

Diocese – the Church in a certain area for which the bishop is responsible

Disciple – 'learner or follower' ; the disciples followed Jesus during his ministry on earth and learnt from him

Divinity – being God

Emmanuel – a name meaning 'God with us', and one of the titles of the Messiah

Eucharist – a service of thanksgiving, frequently used as another name for the Mass or Holy Communion

Evangelical groups – enthusiastic or zealous supporters of a particular cause and very eager to make other people share its beliefs or ideals

Evil One – Satan, the devil

Exorcism – driving out evil, freeing from the grip of sin

Extortion – using force to obtain money or information

Frankincense – a sweet smelling gum burned as incense, a gift for a king

Galilee – the northern Jewish region in which Jesus grew up

Gentiles – not born into the Jewish faith or race, non-Jews

Godparent – someone who promises to help bring a baptised person up as a Christian

Handmaid – a female servant

Haemorrhage – flow of blood

High priest – the senior Jewish leader

Incense – a pleasant smelling gum or spice which is burned as a sign of devotion in a religious ceremony

Indelible mark – a mark that cannot be removed

Iniquity – evil, crime, sin

Israel – God's chosen people, the twelve tribes of descendants of Abraham

Jews, Jewish People – the name of the people of Israel after about 500 BC

Keys to the kingdom – Jesus gave Simon Peter authority and leadership over the Church, symbolised by 'the keys to the kingdom'

Kindred – relations

Lay missionary – a missionary who is not ordained to a particular ministry

Legion of Mary – An association of Catholic lay-people who serve the Church on a voluntary basis; there are over three million active members in almost every country in the world

Leprosy – a tropical disease affecting the skin and nerves and in severe cases causing disfigurement

Loose – to untie, to cancel a law or rule

Loose living – reckless living, out of control, irresponsible

Lowly – simple and small

Magnificat – Mary's song of praise to God after she had been greeted by Elizabeth

Malaria – an infectious disease

Martyr – a 'witness', someone who is willing to stand up for their faith, even if is means death

Mass – a frequently used name for the celebration of the Eucharist

Mediator – a go-between, intermediary

Messiah – the Saviour sent by God to save his people from their sins; the one who would preach the Kingdom of God; it is a Hebrew word meaning 'Anointed One'.

Missionary – someone who goes out to preach and teach about Jesus

Model of faith – an excellent example of one who has absolute trust in God

Monastery – a building in which a group of people with religious vows live together, e.g. monks or nuns

Myrrh – an ointment made from the sap of a tree

Nazareth – a town in Galilee where Jesus was brought up

Nero – a Roman Emperor who in AD 64 began persecuting Christians in Rome

New Testament (NT) – the books of the Bible that deal with the life, death and resurrection of Jesus and all that this means for his followers, the Church

Nostra Aetate – it is the Declaration on the Catholic Church's relation to non-Christian Religions of the Second Vatican Council (1962 - 1965)

Novice – a trainee, someone who has joined a religious order but has not yet taken vows

Novitiate – the part of the convent or monastery where novices live

Old Testament (OT) – the Jewish books of the Bible; they are about the friendship between God and Israel before the time of Jesus

Original Sin – the very first sin, also the sinful tendency that human inherit from the disobedience of Adam and Eve

Pagan – one who does not hold the Christian faith but may believe in many gods of nature, a heathen

Pages in court – servants or attendants to a king

Pentecost – a Jewish feast day, celebrated 50 days after Passover

Pentecost Sunday – a Christian feast day remembering the descent of the Holy Spirit upon the apostles and followers of Jesus

Pharisee – a member of a strict sect of people who observed all the Jewish laws and customs, but often it is a word applied to self-righteous people

Ploughshares – the part of the plough that cuts the soil for the furrow

Pneumonia – an inflammatory disease of the lungs

Pope – a word meaning 'father'; used for the Bishop of Rome and the head of the Catholic Church all over the world

Prevail – triumph, succeed

Proclaim – to speak out or to announce (important news)

Prophecies – messages of divine truth revealing God's will

Prophet – someone who proclaims God's messages; one who speaks by divine inspiration

Redeemed – saved, rescued

Remnant – those that remain after the rest has gone

Repentance – turning to God and being truly sorry

Revelation – God's showing Himself to Israel by His Word in the Bible; Christians believe that Jesus is God's full self-revelation

Roman governor – the senior Roman in an occupied territory; the Emperor's representative

Sabbath – the day of rest; seventh day of the week (Saturday in the Jewish calendar, Sunday for Christians)

Sacrifice – the offering of a person or thing to God, often to make up for sin, and sometimes involving death

Sadducees – members of a Jewish group who belonged to the ruling class and denied the resurrection of the dead

Salvation – being saved, being united to God

Sanctifying grace – the help people receive from God enabling them to be saved

Sanhedrin – the Jewish Great Council, made up of Sadducees, Pharisees and teachers of the law

Saul – St. Paul's name before he was called Paul

Saviour – the One who is to save us from sin

Scapegoat – someone who is made to bear the punishment that should rightly fall on others.

Scribes – those who made and kept copies of the Law and helped interpret the Law

Sects – a denomination of a larger religious group

Stock of Jesse – descendants or ancestors of Jesse

Successor – someone who follows in the footsteps of another, who takes on that person's duties and responsibilities

Supernatural – above ordinary life; the spiritual life with God

Swaddling clothes – strips of cloth wrapped around a baby

Symbol – something simple that leads one to imagine a bigger, more mysterious reality

Synagogue – place for Jewish prayer and learning

Tax collector – one who collected tax for the Romans from the Jews; tax collectors were usually hated and considered to be public sinners

Temple – the central place of worship and sacrifice for the Jews in Jerusalem

Temptation – thoughts that can lead us to sin if we give in to them

Ten Commandments – ten rules for living life to the full given by God through Moses to Israel

Torah – a name for the first five books of the Bible; these books are also known as the Law or Pentateuch

Tradition – knowledge, beliefs and customs that are handed down from one generation to the next

Transform – change

Trials – troubles, hardship

Visitation – Mary's visit to Elizabeth after she had been told the news by the Angel Gabriel

Wisdom – the gift of being able to see things as God sees them; the ability to see the truth

Zechariah – father of John the Baptist and husband of Elizabeth

Nihil obstat: Father Anton Cowan (Censor). **Imprimatur:** Rt. Rev. Alan Hopes, V.G., Auxiliary Bishop in Westminster, 18th March 2009, Feast of St. Cyril of Jerusalem.

The Nihil obstat and Imprimatur are a declaration that the books and contents of the DVD ROM are free from doctrinal or moral error. It is not implied that those who have granted the Nihil obstat and the Imprimatur agree with the contents, opinions or statements expressed.

Design, compilation and format Ian Curtis, First Sight Graphics, www.firstsightgraphics.com. **Design and Text copyright** © 2009 Marcellina Cooney CP. Published 2009 by the Teachers' Enterprise in Religious Education Company Limited, 40 Duncan Terrace, London N1 8AL and the Incorporated Catholic Truth Society, 40-46 Harleyford Road, London SE11 5AY.
Picture research Marcellina Cooney CP and Ian Curtis.
ISBN 978 1 86082 539 2

Theological Adviser: Herbert Alphonso SJ
Curriculum Adviser: Joe Fitzpatrick

Illustrations: © Jenny Williams; © Bob Moulder, © Bob Farley/Graham-Cameron-Illustrations; © Ann Baum, © Sally Launder, © Diane Catchpole, © Anthony Morris/Linda Rogers Associates; © Roger Wade Walker/Beehive Illustration; © David McAllister/nbIllustrations

Acknowledgements
Considerable thanks are due to Andrea Curtis, Martin Earley, Louise McKenna, Paul Maloney and Margaret Smart for proof reading 'The Way' Student's Book.

We are grateful to John McLoughlin, Bangor, N. Ireland, for permission to use details of his stained glass windows through the book.

Permission credits
Cover photo: stained glass window © CWS Design, 9 Ferguson Drive, Lisburn BT28 2EX . Cover Photo: clouds © Artyfree. Page 3 Archbishop Vincent Nichols © Peter Jennings. Page 6 and throughout: squiggle man © N.l. Page 14: Bible © Cornishman. Page 15 and throughout: candle © Hkuchera. Page 22 Village residents flee fighting in Sudan © UN/DPI; Congolese refugee children © Karen Kasmauski/Corbis; Ruvinbo Bungwe's poem permission from Dai Jones, Villiers High School. Page 25 © World Religions Photo Library/R. Schogger. Page 24 and throughout: brass candle holder © Berryspun. Page 26 Internally displaced persons in Kosovo © UN.DPI. Page 29 Prophecy of John's birth © Heinemann /AKG Images. Page 31 Annunciation to Mary, Fra Angelico ©AKG Images. Page 36 Adoration of the Shepherds by Mariano Salvador de Maella (1739-1819) © Rafael Valls Gallery, London/Bridgeman Art Library. Page 37 Adoration of the Kings by Dolci, Carlo (1616 – 1686) © National Gallery. Page 39: Wisemen at Bethlehem © Roberto1977. Page 39: Shepherds of Bethlehem © Clarsen55. Page 39: Christmas bells © Diless. Page 39: Robin © Jyothi. Page 40 illustration adapted from clip art image in One Thousand Gospel Images by Jean-Francois Kieffer, © Les Presses d'Ile de France. Pages 43, 44 © Jesuits Yearbook 2007, with permission from Jose M. de Vera SJ. Page 46 Christ the Consoler by Carl Heinrich Bloch (1834-1890 Danish) © Superstock.co.uk. Page 53: Washing hands © Merlin1. Page 55 © B. Mizen. Page 57 St. John Vianney © CWS Design, photos Marcellina Cooney. Page 58 St. Teresa of Avila, PP Rubens © AKG Images. Page 61 Mother Teresa in Calcutta © Kapoor Baldev/Sygma/Corbis. Page 63 and throughout: Chuch candle burning © Fnalphotos. Page 63: Earth map © Yiannos1. Page 64 photo of Pentecost Fr. James McNicholas. Page 68 Martyrdom of St. Stephen by Antonio Carracci (1589-1618) © National Gallery. Page 69 Conversion of St. Paul by Michelangelo Merisi da Caravaggio (1571-1610) © Bridgeman Art Library; Saul flees Damascus by G. De Sanctis (1829-1911) © Basilica Papale di San Paolo fuori le Mura. Page 71 Domine quo vadis? A. Carracci © AKG Images. Pages 72, 74, 75, 76, 85, 103 by Elizabeth Wang, © Radiant Light. Page 78 Stoning of Paul in Lystra by C. Mariani (1826-1901) © Basilica Papale di San Paolo fuori le Mura. Pages 57, 84, 87, 89, 90, 91, 92, 98, 102 photos © Marcellina Cooney. Page 86 Mille Images d'Eglise, © Jean-Francois Kieffer, Mille Images Symboliques, © Patrick Royer, Les Presses d'Ile de France. Page 94 The Prodigal's Return by John Byam Liston Shaw (1872-1919) © Russell-Cotes Art Gallery and Museum UK/Bridgeman Art Library. Page 95 Return of the Prodigal Son by Spada © AKG-Images. Page 97 © St. Vartan Armenian Church, Canada. Page 101 © moodboard/Corbis. Page 105 Apostle Paul by El Greco © AKG Images. Page 107 Jesuits Yearbook 2006; page 121 Jesuits Yearbook 2008 © permission from Jose M. de Vera SJ. Page 105 Apostle Paul, El Greco © AKG-Images. Page 109 Edel Quinn, © Legion of Mary. Page 114 Inter Faith Centre, St. Gregory's Science College, Cardinal Hinsley High School. Pages 116 Guru Nanak © World Religions Photo Library/Christine Osborne. Page 117 Buddha statue © World Religions Photo Library/Mini Forsyth. Page 120 photo of Cardinal Hume by Bill Gribbin, courtesy of Westminster Cathedral Archives; photo of Rabbi Jonathan Sacks from Anna Sinclair. Page 124 Mahatma Gandhi © Bettmann/Corbis. Page 108 Uganda Martyrs image courtesy of www.CatholicPrayerCards.org.

Every effort has been made to contact copyright holders of material used in this publication. Any omissions will be rectified in subsequent printings if notice is given to the publisher.